THE
SOURCES OF THE
SYNOPTIC GOSPELS

THE
SOURCES OF THE
SYNOPTIC GOSPELS

BY THE LATE
WILFRED L. KNOX, D.D.
FELLOW OF PEMBROKE COLLEGE, CAMBRIDGE
FELLOW OF THE BRITISH ACADEMY

EDITED BY
H. CHADWICK
FELLOW OF QUEENS' COLLEGE, CAMBRIDGE

VOLUME TWO
ST LUKE & ST MATTHEW

CAMBRIDGE
AT THE UNIVERSITY PRESS
1957

PUBLISHED BY
THE SYNDICS OF THE CAMBRIDGE UNIVERSITY PRESS

London Office: Bentley House, N.W.I
American Branch: New York

Agents for Canada, India, and Pakistan: Macmillan

Printed in Great Britain at the University Press, Cambridge
(Brooke Crutchley, University Printer)

CONTENTS

EDITOR'S PREFACE

Some preliminary apology may seem necessary for the delay in the appearance of this second volume. This has been caused partly by pressure of other responsibilities of a less academic nature, but more by the sheer difficulties of its compilation. The making of the book has been in some respects strikingly similar to the process which Dr Knox postulated as a hypothesis to account for the Gospel evidence. The piecing together of short sections, with editorial modifications and additions where only fragmentary notes survived, has been a slow and laborious task. Of necessity some substantial gaps have had to be filled, and I am acutely conscious of the inadequacy of my supplements and alterations, which are all too extensive; if some sections have been left virtually as Dr Knox wrote them, others have been completely rewritten or new matter provided. But it has seemed better to publish this rather than nothing, especially since the persuasiveness of the book's main thesis depends much upon the Lucan evidence, and the first volume on St Mark can hardly stand without it. No attempt, on the other hand, has been made to bring the book up to date with decorative footnotes referring to other contemporary discussions of Gospel origins, except that some fragmentary notes on the Oxyrhynchus Logia have been expanded to take account of certain views advanced by Professor Joachim Jeremias in his *Unbekannte Jesusworte*; but it would have made the editorial task insuperable to have considered his book on *The Parables of Jesus* or Dr Vincent Taylor's learned commentary on St Mark. Some rough outline comments on the problem of Jesus' Messianic consciousness have been made the basis of a brief discussion of the criteria of authenticity, which may serve in part as a reply to certain critics of the first volume, who on the one side suggested that the implications of Dr Knox's book mean an abandonment of the Christian faith, or on the other side that serious historical criticism need take no account of his work as being merely disguised apologetic presented in an oblique form.

H. CHADWICK
April 1955

QUEENS' COLLEGE
CAMBRIDGE

ABBREVIATIONS

Bultmann   *Die Geschichte der synoptischen Tradition*, by R. Bultmann. Second edition, Göttingen, 1931.

Creed   *The Gospel according to St Luke*, by J. M. Creed. London, 1930.

Dibelius   *Die Formgeschichte des Evangeliums*, by M. Dibelius. Second edition, Tübingen, 1933.

F.G.H.   *Die Fragmente der griechischen Historiker*, ed. F. Jacoby. Berlin and Leiden, 1923–50.

Gentiles   *St Paul and the Church of the Gentiles*, by W. L. Knox. Cambridge, 1939.

Hellenistic Elements   *Some Hellenistic Elements in Primitive Christianity*, by W. L. Knox (Schweich Lectures, 1942). London, 1944.

Jerusalem   *St Paul and the Church of Jerusalem*, by W. L. Knox. Cambridge, 1925.

J.T.S.   *Journal of Theological Studies*.

Kilpatrick   *Origins of the Gospel according to St Matthew*, by G. D. Kilpatrick. Oxford, 1946.

P.M.G.   *Papyri Magicae Graecae*, ed. K. Preisendanz.

P.W.K.   Pauly-Wissowa-Kroll, *Realencyclopädie der classischen Altertumswissenschaft.*

Rawlinson   *St Mark*, by A. E. J. Rawlinson. London, 1925.

Smith   *The Parables of the Synoptic Gospels*, by B. T. D. Smith. Cambridge, 1937.

Str.-B.   *Kommentar zum Neuen Testament aus Talmud und Midrasch*, by H. L. Strack and P. Billerbeck. Munich, 1922–28.

Streeter   *The Four Gospels*, by B. H. Streeter. London, 1924.

T.W.z.N.T.   *Theologisches Wörterbuch zum Neuen Testament*, ed. G. Kittel and G. Friedrich.

PART I

THE QUESTION OF Q

CHAPTER I

THE Q TRADITION

Although some have had doubts, it is still generally regarded as almost axiomatic that besides the Gospel of Mark there lay before the compilers of Matthew and Luke another document, described as Q, which contained all that matter which is common to both of them, but not found in Mark. Streeter (pp. 272 ff.) attempts to reconstruct the document; it has even been suggested that Mark himself may have been acquainted with Q.

I have not the smallest intention of doubting that the large amount of material which is common to Matthew and Luke, but is not drawn from Mark, is drawn by them from a common source or group of sources. But it is necessary to insist that Q is simply a hypothetical document; its claim to have existed rests on its being the best hypothesis to explain the fact that there is much material to be found in these two Gospels which shows so close a resemblance of wording (sometimes amounting to complete identity) that it must have been derived by both of them from a common written source, or at least an oral source which was regarded as authoritative and memorized by Christian teachers.

But the document reconstructed out of this common material by Streeter (p. 291) is of a very peculiar character. It begins as a narrative with the ministry of the Baptist, the Baptism of Jesus, the Temptation and the Rejection at Nazareth. Then come the Sermon on the Plain and the story of the centurion's servant, followed by the message of the Baptist to Jesus with slight narrative framework. The rest of the book consists entirely of sayings, and Q ended with an eschatological discourse (xvii. 20–37), followed apparently by the parable of the pounds, presumably intended to console the reader for the delay in the Second Coming.

It is possible that the material assembled by Streeter was once combined into a single document, though motives which led to a compilation of this kind, ending without a story of the Passion, are very hard to find. But there are grave reasons for doubting some of

3

the elements attributed to Q by Streeter. We have no evidence that there were two accounts of the Baptism of Jesus; Luke at iii. 19 f. has a notice of the Baptist's imprisonment which looks as if it had been intended to lead on to vii. 18 with a short note such as Matt. iv. 2 or Luke iv. 14 f. to describe the growing reputation of Jesus as being possibly 'he that should come'. This notice of John's imprisonment has been eliminated by Matthew, since it was out of place before the story of the Baptism. On the other hand Matt. xi. 2 may well preserve the language of the original source, which was simply the story of the Baptist, as against Luke vii. 18. In the story of the Baptism itself (Matt. iii. 13 ff. and Luke iii. 21 f.) we have no evidence of any source but Mark; Matt. iii. 14 f. is the necessary explanation, from the point of view of the later Church, of the fact that Jesus came to be baptized at all.[1] The growth of the miracle in Luke is natural and needs no source, while the substitution of ἀνοιχθῆναι for σχίζεσθαι is simply a stylistic alteration. If Q contained an account of the Baptism it has left no decisive trace. Similarly we have no evidence of a Q story of the rejection at Nazareth. It has been seen above (Vol. 1, pp. 47 ff.) that Luke at iv. 16 ff. has a slightly different version of the Marcan story which he has amplified with a *testimonium* and the sayings about Elijah and Elisha, but we have no proof that his source was anything more than a variant of the Marcan account. The rest of Streeter's material may once have formed a single document, though it is hard to see why it had no story of the Passion. We cannot deny that the primitive Church might have compiled such a collection, but in view of the analysis of Mark in Vol. 1 it seems worth asking whether Q as a single document ever contained more than those elements in which Luke and Matthew employ their common material in the same order, beginning with the appearance of the Baptist[2] and ending with, perhaps,

---

[1] For these difficulties cf. the Gospel of the Ebionites, quoted by Epiph. *Haer.* xxx, 13, and the Gospel according to the Hebrews (Jerome, *c. Pelag.* III, 2). Kilpatrick (*Origins of the Gospel according to St Matthew*, p. 50) is probably right as against Creed (p. 55) in holding that Matthew depends on Mark; he is right in regarding τότε and δικαιοσύνη as Matthean, but χρείαν ἔχω (Matthew 6, Mark 4, and Luke 5) can hardly be so regarded.

[2] Q seems to have contained an account of the Baptist which is responsible (Luke iii. 3 a) for the moderate view of the Baptist's influence as against Mark i. 5 (Matthew abbreviates Q and adds Mark's version at iii. 5). Luke iii. 3b may be the Q version:

the charge to the disciples which Luke gives as a charge to the Seventy, while Matthew conflates it with Mark's charge to the Twelve. Even this document may well have been a chance conflation of shorter tracts, each of which formed in the first place an independent unit.

Since it is generally agreed that Luke on the whole uses his sources in large blocks, while Matthew feels far more free to break them up and readjust them to suit his purpose, it will be safest to start with the Lucan use of the Q material and see how far it shows evidence of having once consisted of smaller units. For this purpose it will be necessary to break up into two sections the material normally attributed to, or designated as, Q: the first consisting of the block of material which is preserved in the main in the same order in both Luke and Matthew, except in cases where Matthew may be supposed to have rejected Q in favour of Mark. In both Gospels other matter has been interpolated from Mark or elsewhere; but both preserve the main outlines of this sequence. The other section consists of those passages common to Luke and Matthew which have no organic connexion of this kind and appear as sayings or groups of sayings in entirely different contexts in the two evangelists.

It is immediately clear that the first of these two sections falls into at least two subdivisions. In the first place we have a description of the opening of the ministry of Jesus with special reference to his relation to the Baptist, followed after a considerable interval in our present Gospels by an account of the Baptist's message to Jesus and Jesus' answer. In Luke the Baptist's message is only divided from the story of the centurion's servant by the story of the widow's son (vii. 11–17), in Matthew by a large block of mainly Marcan material. Its position in Luke seems to be explained by the reasons given below (p. 8, n. 2). But in a tract dealing with the opening of the ministry and the relation of Jesus to the Baptist it would be simple

---

iii. 5 f. is probably Lucan expansion. Luke iii. 7–9 (=Matt. iii. 7–10) will be from Q: iii. 10 ff. might or might not be. It would seem that the core of the Baptist's message from the Christian point of view (Mark i. 7 f. and Luke iii. 16 (=Matt. iii. 11 f.)) stood in an almost identical form in both, apart from the addition of καὶ πυρί in Q. It would appear that a stereotyped version of the message is older than either source: καὶ πυρί will have been added to the Q source or omitted by Mark as unintelligible. Luke iii. 16 (=Matt. iii. 12) is clearly from Q, the wording being almost identical.

to pass from the Baptist's teaching and the baptism of Jesus to the Baptist's message from prison, since the intervening period would be assumed to be known from other sources. The story of the Temptation might well fall into such a document, since it expresses the effect on Jesus of his meeting with the Baptist and his own baptism; it remains possible that the accounts of the baptism and Temptation of Jesus were originally independent.

CHAPTER II

THE SERMON ON THE MOUNT

The second subdivision of the Q material consists of the Sermon on the Mount and the healing of the centurion's servant (Matt. viii. 5 ff. = Luke vii. 2 ff.). In Luke the miracle follows immediately after the Sermon; in Matthew it is divided from it by the Marcan story of the healing of the leper (Mark i. 40 ff.). This Matthean insertion gives a clue to the apparently incongruous way in which a detached miracle has been appended to the Sermon. Its point lies in the pronouncement which closes it: 'I have not found so great faith, no, not in Israel.' This forms a fitting close to the new standard of righteousness of which the Sermon is a summary; it is those who have this kind of faith who are members of the kingdom, not Israel. Matthew, however, by his expansions of the Sermon has made it clear that the Torah of the new kingdom is the fulfilment, not the destruction of the old; and so he transfers the cleansing of the leper from its Marcan position, where it introduces the first group of conflict-stories and shows that the opposition of the Pharisees to Jesus was entirely unjustified, to viii. 1, where it follows immediately on the Sermon and implies that the Jewish Law holds good for the new kingdom, even though the healing of the centurion's servant shows that many may come from the East and the West and enter the kingdom (as proselytes), while many Israelites by birth will be rejected. In doing so Matthew has merely carried on the work of the earlier compiler of this section, who found a collection of sayings of Jesus, dramatized in the form of a sermon delivered on a mountain[1] (possibly with the intention of making it appear as the Torah of the new kingdom), and added to it the story of the centurion's servant to make it clear that the message of Jesus was addressed to the Gentiles no less than to the Jews.

[1] It will be seen that Luke has preserved the Sermon in its original form (see below, pp. 9 ff.) or at least in a more original form than Matthew. But the 'level place' of Luke vi. 17 is hardly explicable except as a correction of the mountain of Matt. v. 1. The 'mountain' implied that the Sermon was the new Torah, as Matthew rightly saw. But for Luke the new giving of the Torah which replaces Sinai is the Day of Pentecost; consequently he transfers the Sermon from 'the mountain' to 'a level place'.

It is of course possible that the idea of adding the story of the centurion's servant as a warning occurred to the original compiler, who united the sayings of the Lucan Sermon into a single document; it is possible that the Sermon contains a historical memory of some peculiarly solemn pronouncement by Jesus and even that this was followed by the incident of healing which lies behind the story as it now stands. On the other hand the story appears in the Fourth Gospel (iv. 46 ff.) with the curious βασιλικός in place of the centurion and with no connexion with any discourse of Jesus; it is at least probable that this evangelist found it as a detached story in his source and that it existed as a detached story before it became an appendix to the Sermon.[1] We are thus left with the Sermon as a collection of sayings; whether any part of them was delivered as a sermon or charge to the disciples on any particular occasion can only be decided on grounds of general probability.[2]

---

[1] Cf. P. Gardner-Smith, *St John and the Synoptic Gospels*, p. 22. Somewhat curiously he fails to note the point which not only confirms his view that the story comes from an independent tradition in the Fourth Gospel, but also shows that it comes from an older stage. The words of Jesus in John iv. 48 preserve accurately the refusal of Jesus to use miracles as evidence of his divine mission, a refusal preserved in Mark viii. 12 and the Q parallel (Luke xi. 29=Matt. xii. 38) and elsewhere. But it is already disappearing in the Synoptic tradition (Mark viii. 19 f.), and the Fourth Gospel is entirely thaumaturgic in its view of miracles (ii. 11, xi. 42, xii. 37, etc.). The saying of Jesus can only be explained as a survival from the evangelist's source; his carelessness in not cutting it out in spite of its inconsistency with his normal attitude need cause no surprise. Cf. Vol. i, p. 55.

[2] To some extent the story of the widow's son at Nain (Luke vii. 11–17) supports the view that the Sermon and the story of the centurion's servant (vi. 20–vii. 10) reached Luke as an independent unit; Luke normally keeps his sources together and uses the gap between the end of one and the beginning of another for the insertion of unattached material. This, however, cannot be pressed here. The story of the Baptist had to be broken off after iii. 19, since Jesus must have some works to his credit before John could hear of them and send his disciples to ask the question of vii. 18 f. (=Matt. xi. 2 f.). It is possible that the story of the widow's son was inserted here to justify the νεκροὶ ἐγείρονται of vii. 22 (=Matt. xi. 5); consequently we cannot rule out the possibility that Luke has here inserted the story into the middle of a connected Q. For the Semitic Greek of the story of the widow's son cf. *Hellenistic Elements*, pp. 1 and 20. The very clumsy περὶ αὐτοῦ suggests that v. 17 came to Luke in his tradition; 'in all Judaea' may be Luke's addition. Matthew merely defers the Baptist's question in order to put in a large block of Marcan material and his version of the Marcan and Q charge to the Twelve (with large additions). Luke's attachment of it to the story of the widow's son and the acclamation which follows it is highly effective.

A. THE LUCAN SERMON

It might indeed be argued that the Matthean Sermon is nearer to the original than the Lucan, Luke having simply omitted the Matthean contrast between the old Torah and the new (Matt. v. 17–48) apart from a few pieces of ethical teaching, and the section on prayer, fasting and almsgiving (Matt. vi. 1–18).[1] An intelligible motive for the former omission is clear: Luke did not regard Christianity as a new version of the Torah. The second omission is again explicable, since it envisages the conditions of the religion of Palestine; public alms-giving, praying and fasting would hardly be intelligible in a Gentile city. Thus, it could be urged, Luke has left only the ethical elements of the sermon, partly on account of his Gentile bias, partly because he wishes to deprive the Sermon of its character of the giving of the new Torah from the new Sinai. There are, however, serious objections to this view.

(1) At Luke vi. 37b–38 we have material which does not appear in Matthew. (There is a considerable difference between Luke vi. 34–6 and Matt. v. 44–8, but here Luke adds nothing, his expansion being purely homiletic, while Matt. v. 45, apart from his change of υἱοὶ ὑψίστου into υἱοὶ τοῦ πατρός κτλ., cf. p. 40, has every claim to be regarded as original rather than Luke vi. 35b.) The picture of the 'good measure heaped and running over', and the Semitic use of the third person plural as meaning 'God',[2] suggest that we have here primitive Palestinian material which Matthew has eliminated, probably by accident, in expanding the Sermon from other sources. This is admittedly not conclusive, since Luke might have found the fuller form of the saying vi. 37–8 elsewhere and put it in the place of the briefer Matthean version which stood in their common source.

(2) It is more important that much of the material in the Lucan Sermon has every claim to be regarded as giving the more primitive position and meaning of the sayings involved than the Matthean. Thus Luke vi. 39 as it stands is a general warning against judging others, reinforced by 40. Both utterances have a character of homely wisdom, which is entirely in keeping with the teaching of Jesus as we find it in many of the parables (cf. Smith, pp. 59f.). But in

---

[1] Cf. the various views quoted by Creed, p. 90.
[2] Cf. *Hellenistic Elements*, p. 9.

Matthew the saying of Luke vi. 39 appears not here but at xv. 14, where it reinforces the condemnation of the Pharisees, regarded as the conventional villains of the piece (cf. also Matt. xxiii. 16 and 24). They clearly do not belong to this context, since the section as a whole is taken over from Mark (Matt. xv. 1–20=Mark vii. 1–23). The section is omitted by Luke, whose readers are not interested in the discussion of Jewish rules of ceremonial purity, although he has included the denunciations of the Pharisees (xi. 37–52 and xx. 45–7, for which cf. Vol. I, pp. 93 ff.). But it can hardly be supposed that Matthew had a version of the Corban story from Q in which the warning against 'blind guides' appeared, and that Luke, while omitting the incident, has transferred the warning to its present position and watered it down into the homely wisdom of vi. 39. In the same way vi. 40 in its Lucan position is a saying of a similar character; the best that a disciple can hope for is that in the end he may be as good as his master. But Matthew has transferred it to x. 24 where it appears as an encouragement to the disciple to persevere in the face of persecution; it is to be presumed that the saying in this sense had a wide circulation in the Church, in view of John xiii. 16 and xv. 20. But again it is very unlikely that Luke would have watered it down.[1]

(3) It is yet more significant that Luke vi. 39 opens with the words 'And he spake also a parable unto them'. Obviously such an insertion is out of place in a sermon; there is no such introduction to the far more elaborate parable of the two houses, and no similar introduction in the Matthean Sermon. We have here a survival from the period when a 'sermon' was a collection of sayings each with its introduction 'And he said' (or words to similar effect); the original compiler, who made a sermon out of a collection of sayings, has forgotten to cut out the words and Luke has left them intact.[2]

[1] It is of course possible that Jesus used words of this kind on more than one occasion and with different meanings. Matt. x. 25b has a distinctly primitive character and may well be a genuine saying. 'It is enough for the disciple that he is as his master' has parallels in early rabbinical literature, cf. *Genesis Rabba* 49 (30d) quoted by Str.-B. on Matt. x. 24.

[2] It would be possible to hold that Luke had before him the 'sermon' without vi. 39–40, which came to him as a floating 'parable', and inserted them here with their narrative introduction. But it is far more likely that he would leave the clumsy bit of narrative if he found it in his source, in view of his general carelessness in revision, than that he would leave it if he was inserting the whole passage into an existing source.

(4) Luke vi. 43–5 has been treated by Matthew in the same way as Luke vi. 39 f. Again we have a piece of homely wisdom: 'a good tree cannot bear bad fruit'. Matthew has written up this group of sayings and used it twice.[1] He has transferred it from its Lucan position after vi. 42 (= Matt. vii. 5) to vii. 16 where it stands in the eschatological conclusion which follows the Golden Rule, and changed it from a saying of general application to a warning against false prophets; the contrast between good and bad treasures of Luke vi. 45 is omitted and replaced by a pronouncement of the doom of the false prophets modelled on the language of John the Baptist. But the contrast between trees and their fruits was too good to be left out in dealing with the Pharisees, and the matter is repeated at Matt. xii. 33 as an addition to the reply to the charge of casting out devils by Beelzebub. Once again it is amplified with language reminiscent of the Baptist, who appears to have left a tradition of invective which the Jewish Church found invaluable in its controversy with the rest of the nation.

It is thus fairly clear that the Lucan form of the Sermon is nearer the original, and that it had passed through the form of a collection of independent sayings and been changed into a sermon before it reached either evangelist. It is indeed possible that in the pre-canonical form the Sermon included the document dealing with the new Torah, the duties of prayer, fasting and almsgiving and a further triad of sayings which cannot be traced with certainty,[2] and that Luke simply cut it out as being of interest only for Jewish readers; and this view can be supported by the fact that Luke found the Sermon in the form of a new Torah and deliberately deprived it of that character (cf. above, p. 7, n. 1). The Sermon would look more like a new Torah with those sections than without them. We cannot rule out the possibility that Luke has omitted this block of

[1] For an amusing instance of a double use of the same quotation from a source cf. Plutarch, *Themistocles*, x and XXXII. In x Plutarch, following Phylarchus, describes how Themistocles exploited various prodigies to persuade the Athenians to leave the city ὥσπερ ἐν τραγῳδίᾳ μηχανὴν ἄρας; he goes on to describe the departure in highly dramatic language, which is probably drawn from Phylarchus. But in XXXII Plutarch criticizes the same author for his melodramatic inventions with regard to the sons of Themistocles ὥσπερ ἐν τραγῳδίᾳ τῇ ἱστορίᾳ μονονοὺ μηχανὴν ἄρας. He thus uses Phylarchus' own words to condemn him after using them with apparent approval at x. Cf. *F.G.H.* 81, F 22 and Jacoby's notes *ad loc.*

[2] For this source cf. below, pp. 20 ff.

material. In any case the point is of secondary importance for our purpose. The matter in question by its whole character reveals itself as having originally formed an independent tract. This tract may have been combined with the rest of the Lucan material to form the sermon on the new Torah before it reached the evangelists and then omitted by Luke and retained by Matthew, or it may have existed as an independent unit until Matthew, or an earlier editor, combined it with the rest of the discourse. In either case in the first instance it had an existence of its own. For the rest it is fairly clear that the Lucan form of the Sermon is on the whole more original, and that the sayings of which it is made up had been combined into a 'sermon' before they reached the evangelists; this sermon opened with the Beatitudes and ended with the parable of the two houses.

Here, however, we are faced with the difficulty of the different form of the Beatitudes in Matthew and Luke. In Matt. v. 3 ff. we have eight, Matt. v. 11 being rather an expansion of 10 than a separate beatitude.[1] In Luke we have also an ogdoad, with four blessings and four woes. The number eight is probably a fixed part of the tradition; the Lucan version in its more concrete form ('the poor' as against the 'poor in spirit', 'those who hunger' as against 'those who hunger and thirst after righteousness', those who mourn shall 'laugh' as against 'be comforted') seems nearer the original, the Matthean version being modified so as to give the spiritual meaning, though it is also possible that Luke's source has been influenced by the literal insistence on poverty of the primitive Jewish Church. This is a question which can hardly be decided except on subjective grounds. The important point is that while we have every reason to

---

[1] Creed on Luke vi. 23 suggests that the woes were perhaps not part of Luke's source. But they were certainly not invented by Luke in view of the extreme clumsiness of the variation between the dative in vi. 24, the dative with the vocative in apposition in 25 a, and the vocative in 25 b. Moreover, Luke only uses οὐαί where he is following a source which uses inferior Greek (x. 13=Matt. xi. 21; xi. 42–52 from the same source as Matt. xxiii. 25 ff.; for xvii. 1 and xxii. 22 cf. *Hellenistic Elements*, p. 22; xxi. 23=Mark xiii. 17). The word οὐαί is not necessarily Semitic (cf. Moulton-Milligan, *Voc. Gr. N.T.* s.v.), but it is by no means clear that Luke would have used it and it may be regarded as certain that he would not have used it with such a clumsy variety of cases to follow. On the other hand the contrast between blessings and woes is rabbinical (cf. Yoma 87a). This need not prove that they are original, since they may be due to the oral tradition of the Church of Palestine through which they have passed; but it is fairly clear that Luke is quoting directly from his source without troubling to revise it.

suppose that the main body of the collection of sayings which forms the Sermon is derived by both evangelists from a common source, the Beatitudes appear to have reached them in different forms. Thus it would appear that we have to allow for a further stage in the tradition; we have (a) the collection of sayings, (b) the presentation of the collection of sayings as a 'sermon', and (c) the addition of the Beatitudes from oral tradition but in two different forms.[1] It is only after this that we reach (d) the use of the Sermon by the evangelists. The probability that the Sermon once began without the Beatitudes is confirmed by the fact that Luke vi. 27 opens with the words 'But I say unto you that hear'. The words are natural and appropriate as a transition from the woes on the absent 'rich' to the faithful to whom the Sermon is addressed, though it is at least possible that in the original collection of sayings there was a clause to the effect that 'Jesus said unto his disciples', which has been changed by the compiler of the Sermon into 'But I say unto you'. At Matt. xix. 24 'Again I say unto you' replaces Mark's statement that the disciples were amazed and that 'again Jesus answered and said unto them' (Mark x. 24).[2] This point cannot be regarded as certain, since we have a good connexion of sense joining the last Beatitude to the theme of loving your enemies.

The Sermon passes at Luke vi. 39 from the command not to judge others as part of the law of love to the folly of judging the imperfections of others when you are imperfect yourself, and from this to the impossibility of producing good fruit from a bad tree;[3]

[1] Kilpatrick (*Origins*, pp. 16ff.) suggests that the Beatitudes of Matt. v. 5, 7, 8 and 9 were originally simple sayings, *v.* 5 being a quotation of Ps. xxxvi. 11. I cannot agree with his view that the use of διώκω in v. 10 and 11 need be due to Matthew's editing. Matthew uses it six (or seven) times, Luke twice. But it appears in Acts vii. 52, xxii. 4, xxvi. 11, twice in the story of Paul's conversion which is repeated three times, and it is frequent in Paul. Thus the word cannot be regarded as specially 'Matthean'.

[2] Ἐγὼ δὲ λέγω ὑμῖν in Matt. v. 22, etc., is of course necessitated by the contrast between the old Torah and the new. The transition at Luke vi. 27 would be abrupt without it, but not more abrupt than the transitions at Luke vi. 38–45, with the changes from the second person plural to the singular and back again (no doubt because we have a collection of sayings originally uttered on quite separate occasions).

[3] Possibly the saying about trees and fruits has been preserved in a form nearest to the original in Matt. vii. 16, in view of the resemblance between this and Jas. iii. 12, where, however, it is the fig that cannot bear olives nor the vine figs. This change may be due to the influence of popular philosophy (cf. Plut. *De Tranq. Anim.* XIII,

thereafter we pass to the theme of the good and bad treasures of the heart, limited by the last clause of vi. 45 to sins of speech. Here we are dealing with a connexion of verbal association rather than of logical development; the mention of the imperfect man who judges others leads to a general contrast between the good and the bad man. It is probable that the last clause of vi. 45 was originally a separate saying since the contrast of the preceding verses should cover a wider field than sins of speech. In Matthew the contrast between trees and fruits has a wider reference in vii. 16 ff., where it has been transferred to the warning against false prophets (cf. above, p. 11), the contrast between good and bad treasures being omitted, presumably because the false prophet has no treasure at all. But the contrast was too good to be wasted and so Matthew employs it again at xii. 33 ff. as a warning against the Pharisees (cf. above, p. 11); here the contrast of good and bad treasures appears, for the Pharisees have a treasure, but it is a bad one. Here also we have the limitation to sins of speech, but this is appropriate in a condemnation of the Pharisees as teachers. But both Matthean contexts are secondary: the lack of organic connexion in Luke represents the original collection of sayings from which both are drawing.

That both are using the same collection in the same, or practically the same, form is clear from the amount of verbal agreement,[1] except at points where Matthew's adaptation of the matter necessitates a change or where we find minor stylistic variations. Thus Luke vi. 27–8 has been abbreviated by Matt. v. 44 (the longer form of the Caesarean texts being due to assimilation); Matthew has changed the more primitive ἐπηρεαζόντων implying ill-treatment of any kind to διωκόντων in view of the experience of the primitive Church. Matthew's version of the saying in Luke vi. 29 (= Matt.

472 F), and intended to modify the original language as too grotesque for Greek taste. If so, however, the comparison is not really to the point; it should be that the vine cannot bear both grapes and thorns (cf. Bonhöffer, *Epiktet u. d. N.T.* pp. 92 f.). The writer of the Epistle of James may have been influenced by the commonplace as heard from wandering cynic preachers. On the other hand he confines the saying to sins of speech, which may mean that he has both Matthean passages before him and that the resemblance of form to Matt. vii. 16 is accidental.

[1] For an example of quite wide variation in the transcription of a common original cf. the passage of Theopompus given in Polybius, VIII, 11, 5–13, and Athenaeus, VI, 77, 260 D (printed in parallel columns by Jacoby, *F.G.H.* 115, F 225).

v. 39–40) is prefaced with 'But I say unto you' in accordance with his general scheme (for this see below, pp. 20 ff.). Luke in general appears to have preserved the rhythm of the original saying better than Matthew (cf. below, p. 16, n. 1): his substitution of τῷ τύπ-τοντί σε πάρεχε for ὅστις σε ῥαπίζει … στρέψον αὐτῷ represents a harmless improvement of the style; and he is nearer the original in representing the taking of the coat as a piece of highway robbery, not as a legal process. Luke omits the ἀγγαρεία and μίλιον of Matt. v. 41 from dislike of the barbarisms, but the saying at Luke vi. 30, with its absolute command to give to all who ask and not to ask your own back from those who rob you, has been decidedly softened down by Matthew. There is a considerable difference between Luke vi. 32–5 a and Matt. v. 45 f.; Matthew may have abbreviated, while Luke vi. 34 f. reads like a homiletic expansion. The difference may in part be due to the fact that Matthew is follow-ing a version of these sayings which had been coloured by a bitterly anti-Gentile attitude (see below, pp. 32 ff.). He has transferred the matter of Luke vi. 35 b (= Matt. v. 45) to the beginning of his section on loving your enemies; here Matthew seems to have preserved a more original form of the saying (below, p. 16, n. 1), but he has probably altered 'merciful' in Luke vi. 36 to 'perfect' (cf. Creed's note *ad loc.*). Matthew has cut down Luke vi. 37 drastically, but with only slight verbal modifications in what remains (cf. below, p. 16, n. 1).

So far the variations might conceivably be due to differences in the sources followed by the evangelists; but in the piece which follows the variations are negligible. Luke has sixty-nine words and Matthew sixty-five (Luke vi. 41–2 = Matt. vii. 3–5); of these fifty-eight are common to both and the differences are readily explicable as due to a normal Lucan improvement in the style (τὴν ἐν τῷ ἰδίῳ and αὐτὸς τὴν ἐν τῷ ὀφθαλμῷ σου δοκὸν οὐ βλέπων): in any case they are trifling. This measure of agreement here, and the ease with which most of the alterations can be accounted for, make it reasonably safe to assume that apart from Matt. v. 46 f. both Matthew and Luke are using the same source throughout: we must bear in mind that some of the differences may be caused by the fact that it came to them in slightly different forms. The wide differences in the saying about trees and their fruits, and the changes in the order, are to be explained by the fact that Matthew has altered its position to fit it into the structure of his Sermon, while Luke on the other hand has abbreviated. Probably the original document simply stated that Jesus 'said', or 'spake another parable saying', and then gave the words of Jesus in the form and order of Matt. vii. 16b–18 (16a is either a Matthean connexion or the ending of the warning of 15, which furnished him with a link for connecting trees and their fruits with false prophets). The vigorous question and the Semitic parallelism have an original air, while Luke reads like a summary of the Matthean form; on the other hand Matthew's use of ἀγαθός and πονηρός as well as καλός and σαπρός to describe the trees and their fruits is probably his own variation due to the ethical meaning of the parable; it does not appear in his parallel use of the saying in xii. 33 ff. The saying concerning good and evil treasures has been transferred to this point in Matthew as noted above, and the words 'out of the abundance of the heart the mouth speaketh', which may originally have been added by the compiler as a summary of the whole series of sayings (Luke vi. 39–45), have been put by Matthew between the good and evil trees and the good and evil treasures to serve as a link for connecting the two. Here again we have only editorial manipulation and no evidence of a different source. Similarly the next verse in Luke (vi. 46) has a very different form in Matthew.[1] 'It is hard to say whether Matthew has expanded (Wellh., Bultmann) or Luke has abbreviated' (Creed *ad loc.*). In the closing parable Matthew is clearly more original in describing the peasant's hut rather than a well-built house.

[1] Kilpatrick (*Origins*, p. 23) suggests that the language of vii. 21 ('largely made up of stock Matthean phrases') and the more sharply antithetic form of the clauses may be due to Matthew's editing of the shorter Lucan saying. But the fact that Matthew uses the phrase ἐλεύσεται ... οὐρανῶν on three other occasions (v. 20, xviii. 3, xix. 23), and ὁ ποιῶν ... οὐρανοῖς twice (xii. 50 and xxi. 31), hardly justifies the description of them as 'stock Matthean phrases', except in so far as they include the terms 'the kingdom of heaven' and 'my father which is in heaven', which represent Matthew's preference for the periphrasis instead of the direct use of the word 'God' where Matthew may quite well be nearer the original language of Jesus than Mark or Luke. (For rabbinical references to 'doing the will' of God cf. Allen, *ad loc.*) The antithetic form which emphasizes the importance of the precept may just as well be original and the Lucan version an abbreviation as vice versa. For antithetic parallelism as a mark of the Wisdom tradition in Jewish literature and in the teaching of Jesus cf. Burney, *The Poetry of Our Lord*, pp. 71 ff.

It is possible that the Semitic use of rhythm in the sayings of Jesus is due to the evangelists and is not original. (This appears to be implied by Kilpatrick, *Origins*,

Accordingly, we have fairly clear and consistent explanations for the variations which occur and no evidence that the evangelists are following different sources. This increases the probability that the original collection of sayings did not include any Beatitudes, since it is hard to account for such wide variations in so solemn and formal a pronouncement if it always formed the introduction to the 'new Torah'. On the other hand once the original collection had been cast into the form of a sermon, the sermon might well attract the Beatitudes to itself as a suitable opening. But if the Beatitudes had already circulated independently in oral tradition, different churches would naturally demand the retention of the form with which they were familiar.

B. THE MATTHEAN SERMON

Thus the basis of the Sermon on the Mount is the material of the Lucan Sermon; it has been expanded freely with matter drawn from other parts of the source or sources common to Luke and Matthew. To this material has been added the new Torah (unless Luke has cut it out), and at least one other source which can be identified with a high degree of probability, as well as material from Mark.

The Beatitudes are followed in Matthew by the solemn warning of the responsibility of disciples, contained in the sayings on salt and light (v. 13 f.). The first of these is based on a saying which appeared both in Mark and in the Q stratum; the longer form of Matt. v. 13 and Luke xiv. 33 f. must come from a different source

p. 75.) But in practice it is sometimes Luke who preserves the parallelism or the rhythm characteristic of Semitic writing, and not Matthew. It can hardly be supposed that Luke would have been capable of imitating Semitic style in this degree or would have thought it desirable to do so. For a case of Lucan watering down cf. Matt. v. 45, which is lamentably weakened in Luke vi. 35 b (perhaps the original saying was too anthropomorphic for his taste). On the other hand Luke vi. 27–9 preserves a rhythmical structure which Matthew has spoilt by transferring the first verse to v. 44 and inserting 'right' before 'cheek' and 'go to law with thee' in v. 39–40 (cf. Burney, op. cit. p. 114). Thus it may be doubted whether even the compiler of Matthew is himself responsible for the rhythm and parallelism of the sayings of Jesus; he may have had rather more feeling for Semitic methods of writing than Luke and on the whole preserved these elements better; but it seems doubtful whether he would have introduced them deliberately in view of the fact that on some occasions he eliminates them. Cf. Matthew's omission of Mark viii. 38 at xvi. 26: the effect is to spoil the Marcan parallelism as effectively as Luke has done (ix. 26) by omitting ἐν τῇ γενεᾷ ταύτῃ τῇ μοιχαλίδι καὶ ἁμαρτωλῷ.

from the isolated logion of Mark ix. 50. In both Mark and Luke the sayings stand without any organic connexion with their context (cf. below, p. 88); it is therefore fairly safe to infer that their position in Matthew is artificial and due to the evangelist. The saying on light appears in Mark iv. 21 as an insertion into his 'tract of parables' (cf. Vol. I, pp. 35 ff.), and Luke (viii. 16) preserves it in that position. Luke, however, also has the saying at xi. 33 immediately after a block of Q material (the sayings on the Queen of the South and the sign of Jonah) with which it has no connexion. Luke has largely rewritten the Marcan version (Luke viii. 16 f. = Mark iv. 21) on the lines of his other version (xi. 33 οὐδεὶς λύχνον ἅψας ... ἵνα οἱ εἰσπορευόμενοι βλέπωσιν), and this version seems to have influenced Matt. v. 13 as well (note the active καλοῦσιν and τιθέασιν, and λάμπει πᾶσιν τοῖς ἐν τῇ οἰκίᾳ). It is possible that the saying reached Luke already in its present position, but its placing between the end of the sayings on the Queen of the South and the sign of Jonah and the denunciation of the Pharisees suggests that it was an isolated saying which he inserted at a gap between his sources. Thus it would seem that Matthew conflated the Marcan and Q versions and inserted them here, while Luke revised the Marcan on the lines of the Q version in order to avoid the obscurity of the Marcan μήτι ἔρχεται and to provide a rather more imposing house; presumably he retained the Q version and inserted it at xi. 33 (though it is simply a doublet of viii. 16) either out of sheer carelessness or because xi. 33 was already attached to 34–6 and these latter sayings carried 33 with them. Matt. v. 14b, concerning the city set on a hill, looks like an isolated saying inserted here by the evangelist; it has no parallel in Luke, we have no clue to its original context and, while it is proverbial in form, there seems no evidence of a parallel in Jewish or Hellenistic literature.[1]

---

[1] Wetstein *ad loc.* quotes Cicero, *Cat.* IV, 6 'Videor enim mihi hanc urbem videre, lucem orbis terrarum atque arcem omnium gentium', which is interesting in view of the not very obvious association of a city and a light of the world. It is conceivable that there was a similar conception of Jerusalem as a city whose position on the hills corresponded to its possession of the Torah which qualified it to be the light of the world, or to become the light of the world in the Messianic age; but there seems to be no evidence to this effect. If so, one would be inclined to suppose that the saying is drawn from Christian circles in which the Church is the true Jerusalem, as in Gal. iv. 26, and the Jerusalem community the true Church; but this is entirely hypothetical.

At v. 17 Matthew provides an introduction to his main non-Lucan source, the new Christian Torah (cf. above, p. 11), an exposition of the outlook of Jewish Christianity. This introduction is based on the saying which appears as an isolated sentence at Luke xvi. 17, where it forms part of the marginal gloss inserted probably by the evangelist himself, after the bulk of his Gospel had been committed to writing (cf. below, p. 98). The saying has been expanded by its eschatological conclusion, intended perhaps to answer the view of some Christians that the Law had ceased to be valid since the Messianic age had begun, a view for which support could be found in the rabbinical speculations as to how far the Torah would be valid in the Messianic age.[1]

Matt. v. 19 appears to be an isolated saying. Kilpatrick (*Origins*, p. 17) rightly points out that the phrase 'these commandments', as the verse stands, has nothing to refer to, and suggests that originally it stood after 41 in Matthew's source with 20 following it as an introduction to vi. 1. In this case we should no longer have to understand 19 f. as referring to the Law, a reference which has always proved a difficulty. But the proposed transference involves difficulties. One would expect Matthew to notice the awkwardness; and it is a more serious difficulty that to be called least in the kingdom of heaven for breaking one of the least commandments and teaching men to do so is a serious anticlimax if the document had already warned those who merely broke one of them of the danger of hellfire. The real problem is to identify the person or persons who are 'in the kingdom of God' and yet 'least' in it. It would seem that the saying is drawn from a moderate Jewish-Christian source which recognizes that Paul and his Gentile converts are in the kingdom of heaven, but 'least' in it, forming something of an inferior

---

[1] For such speculations cf. Str.-B. *ad loc.*; H. J. Schoeps, *Aus frühchristlicher Zeit* (1950), pp. 221 ff. Such a view may have been put forward by the early Hellenist converts, cf. *Jerusalem*, c. 2, n. 10. It could naturally be inferred from the thought of the new creation of all things in Christ as in II Cor. v. 17. The phrase ἕως ἂν πάντα γένηται appears to be a secondary Christian way of referring to the Second Coming; cf. the modification of Mark xiii. 30, where we read that heaven and earth will not pass away till the preceding prophecies have been fulfilled, a saying modified in Luke xxi. 32 where 'this generation' shall not pass away until 'all things are fulfilled' by the Second Coming. Here we have the same use of a phrase which has become conventional.

caste.[1] Matt. v. 20 again, while it would serve as an introduction to vi. 1 ff., could hardly follow on v. 19. The scribes and Pharisees might be charged with 'saying and not doing', but hardly with teaching men not to keep the least of the commandments. On the whole it would seem most likely that 19–20 originally stood as the introduction to the section of the Sermon which follows; it is probable that in their original form the sayings were introduced with 'Jesus said' or a similar formula.

The source itself can be reconstructed with some confidence. It began with three expositions of the new Torah, each with a similar structure. Each began with the formula 'Ye have heard that it was said . . . but I say unto you'. This was followed by a sentence or two of interpretation, and ended with the warning against the danger of hell-fire; in the third the warning is that anything more than 'yea, yea' and 'nay, nay' is from the evil one, but, as will be seen, there is reason to suspect that this passage has been considerably modified in transmission. In each of the three groups of sayings (Matt. v. 21–6, 27–30, and 33–7) we have a genuine re-interpretation of a specific commandment of the Decalogue, which extends its scope from a prohibition of acts which disobey the letter to a condemnation of all thoughts and words which are contrary to the spirit of the commandment; each ends with a warning.

The original form, however, has been considerably modified. Apart from the difficulties of Matt. v. 22 b (on which see the commentaries *ad loc.*) two sayings have been added to the original, 23 f. on leaving your gift before the altar, and 25 f. on agreeing with your adversary. Of these the first would appear to go back to the period when Jewish Christians are still offering sacrifices in the Temple and regard such sacrifices as their chief act of worship. The second, 25 f., appears at Luke xii. 58 f., where it concludes a collection of warnings which begins at 49; both this and the pre-

---

[1] I owe the suggestion to Professor Dodd. The saying of Matt. xiii. 52 seems to reflect the same point of view. The ideal Christian is the converted scribe who combines the exposition and practice of the old Torah with the exposition and practice of the new. Matt. v. 19 in its present form can hardly be authentic; xiii. 52 may well preserve a genuine record of Jesus' hopes of converting the religious leaders and his pleasure at finding one or more scribes among his followers at some early period of his ministry. Such sayings may have been preserved in the oral tradition of Jewish-Christian circles, not in a written document.

ceding warning on judging the signs of the times as you would judge the weather (Luke xii. 54–6) may in the first instance have been warnings against the growing opposition to Rome, the 'adversary' being here the power of the Roman empire. It may, however, simply be a warning to face the crisis produced in the world by the appearance of Jesus.[1] The Lucan position is more original; an isolated saying of the Q tradition has been placed by Matthew at this point to enforce the new interpretation of the Sixth Commandment.

The next revision of the Decalogue, the Seventh Commandment, presents the difficulty that Matt. v. 29 and 30 reappear at Mark ix. 43, and are reproduced with some abbreviations by Matthew (xviii. 8 f.) in their Marcan context. The wording of the two Matthean passages, however, is very different and there is hardly more verbal agreement than the minimum necessary for expressing the same thought; both versions display good Semitic parallelism. It would be tempting to suppose that Matthew used the Marcan sayings here to expand the revision of the Seventh Commandment, and then inadvertently forgot to cut them out from their Marcan context when he came to it. But the structure of v. 27 ff. demands some expansion of 28 to preserve the balance with the parallel revisions of the Decalogue in v. 22 and 35. On the other hand, while v. 29 is appropriate here, v. 30 is not.[2] The sayings have no claim to belong to their Marcan context, where they are merely appended to the sayings on scandalizing little ones in the preceding verses on the principle of verbal

---

[1] Cf. Dodd, *Parables of the Kingdom*, pp. 137 ff.

[2] Cf. B. T. D. Smith *ad loc.* in the *Cambridge Greek Testament: St Matthew*. Kilpatrick (*Origins*, pp. 18–19) suggests that 30 should be omitted with Dsyr.sin., a few minuscules and one MS. each of the Old Latin, Vulgate, bohairic and sahidic versions. I cannot share his general confidence in Dsyr.sin. and the Western texts, and it seems more likely that the verse was omitted as inappropriate here and found elsewhere in Matthew than that it was inserted by assimilation to Matt. xviii. 9, since Matt. xviii. 8 f. the hand and foot come before the eye while here they come after. Certainly the passage is easier if the verse be omitted.

The differences in wording between this passage and Mark ix. 43 might all be due to Matthean editing of Mark as Kilpatrick suggests, but I cannot agree that the figures he gives are striking enough to be decisive here. Thus the facts that συμφέρειν appears only three times in Matthew, not in the other Gospels, and that Matthew uses δεξιός eleven times as against Mark's six and Luke's six are not sufficient to be evidential; in any case Matthew is as likely to have edited an independent version of the saying from another source.

association. It would seem that v. 29 always belonged to the document containing the original form of the revised Decalogue; if the sayings go back to Jesus himself, this will always have stood here. But the saying became detached from its original context and triplicated for the sake of a round completeness, and so found its way into the collection of sayings which Mark has incorporated at ix. 41 ff. (cf. Vol. I, pp. 67 f.). Once again we have evidence of a long history behind the sayings in their present form.

The revision of the Seventh Commandment is further expanded by the addition of the Christian 'law of divorce' (Matt. v. 31–2). The importance of this gave it a wide circulation. Mark (x. 10) introduces it as a private explanation given to the disciples 'in the house' after the discussion of divorce with the Pharisees, although there is no need for such an explanation. Luke inserts it in his marginal gloss at xvi. 18 (cf. below, p. 98), while Matthew besides inserting it here also reproduces it at xix. 9 in its Marcan position (x. 11–12);[1] his introduction contrasts it with the old Torah but betrays the fact that it is his own insertion, or at any rate a later expansion of the original form of the new Torah, by the change of the opening formula (ἐρρέθη δέ). As a piece of literary design the whole passage 31 f., standing as it does after 28 ff., is a bad anticlimax.

The next section (Matt. v. 33–7) reverts to the proper opening formula; it does not actually quote the Decalogue in the form of Exod. xx. 7 or Lev. xix. 2 but gives an interpretation of it on the lines of Num. xxx. 3. Here, however, there follows a change of the construction of the revised Torah: instead of 'But I say unto you that whosoever . . .', we have simply the direct prohibition 'I say unto you, Swear not at all'. The change is made all the more curious by the fact that we have teaching on swearing in the 'whosoever' form at Matt. xxiii. 20, and that this teaching deals with the

---

[1] The Marcan and Lucan versions with their absolute prohibition seem clearly original as against the Matthean concession. The saying of Mark x. 11 f. and its parallel is apparently a rule of the Church based on the interpretation of x. 5 ff. It is possible that the Jewish Church could afford to be less rigorous in the matter than the Gentile Churches, since divorce was not on the whole a serious problem in Judaism as it was in the Gentile world (cf. Moore, *Judaism*, II, pp. 123 ff.). In any case the original form of the saying cannot be decided by modern views on the question of divorce.

performance of promises made on oath and condemns the methods of casuistry by which the performance of oaths could be evaded. In other words it is really teaching on the matter of the opening formula of Matt. v. 33, whereas the teaching of 34 f. does not deal necessarily with the use of oaths in connexion with promises, but with swearing in support of statements of any kind.[1] The question is therefore raised whether the original source did not contain a condemnation of rabbinical casuistry along the lines of Matt. xxiii. 16 ff. If so, it may well have seemed not to be sufficiently important to claim a place in the new Torah, especially after the fall of Jerusalem when there was no temple with gold in it and no altar to swear by. Hence Matthew or an earlier reviser of the new Torah has replaced a condemnation of rabbinical casuistry at this point with a general prohibition of swearing drawn from another source. The condemnation of casuistry was transferred to the denunciation of the Pharisees, no doubt with considerable amplifications (cf. Vol. I, pp. 93 ff.), while the prohibition of swearing, also with amplifications, was inserted into the new Torah. In the course of the transference an original ending of the condemnation of casuistry, with a warning of the danger of hell-fire, was lost, the danger of being ἐκ τοῦ πονηροῦ being presumably regarded as equivalent. Thus originally the prohibition of swearing was probably not part of this source: but it contains sayings which the compiler honestly

---

[1] Kilpatrick, *Origins*, p. 20, disputes the general view that the two sayings, one on vows, the other on oaths, have been run together, on the grounds that ὅρκος cannot have the same meaning as εὐχή and that διδόναι ὅρκον can simply mean 'to swear'. It seems, however, to be impossible to explain the dative which follows; it certainly cannot mean 'you shall swear by the Lord'. Nor is it clear what the reference to the Old Testament might be. There seems little doubt that we have a reference to the fulfilment of promises confirmed by oath as in Num. xxx. 3, in which case there is the confusion of thought (pointed out by Allen *ad loc.*) between the necessity of performing promises made on oath, and therefore made to God, and the duty of abstaining from swearing altogether. For the frequent confusion of oaths (promises to do something, confirmed by an oath) and vows (to abstain from something, as having been dedicated to God), cf. S. Liebermann, *Greek in Jewish Palestine*, pp. 177 ff., who does not note that the Christian refusal to swear by the *genii* of the Caesars and their willingness to swear by their safety (Tert. *Apol.* 32; cf. 35) are simply explained by the fact that the former act implied a recognition of the divinity of the emperor or at least of his *daemon*. See also the remarks of Origen, *c. Cels.* VII, 65, who reflects contemporary discussions of the oath's meaning and reviews various opinions, including those of sceptical philosophers to whom it was a piece of innocuous meaninglessness.

and, quite probably, correctly believed to be derived from Jesus[1] himself.

These groups of sayings are followed by two more (Matt. v. 38 ff. and 43 ff.), which are on the surface revisions of the Torah, in so far as they retain the opening structure 'Ye have heard . . . but I say unto you'. But they consist simply of matter drawn from the Lucan Sermon where they have no such introduction (Luke vi. 29 f., 35 b and 32 f.). Moreover, they are not regarded as a binding obligation to inflict retaliation in kind for an injury,[2] while here the *lex talionis* proper is not in question but its extension to cover cases of insult. The second is not even a direct quotation from the Old Testament; it would appear to be a piece of popular morality in the form of a proverb (cf. Str.-B. *ad loc.*). It has been noted that the matter of the two sections appears to be drawn from the Q Sermon as found in Luke. On the other hand, while the variations between Luke vi. 29 f. and Matt. v. 39–41 are easily to be explained on stylistic grounds, the differences between the Lucan and Matthean versions at Matt. v. 44 ff. and Luke vi. 32 ff. seem, as has been noted above (p. 16, n. 1), to imply a different and superior source for Matthew. Matthew's form seems nearer the original in certain respects since the parallelism and the interrogative form, as well as the greater terseness, suggest that Luke has undergone homiletic expansion; nevertheless Matthew has substituted for the original source a variation of the sayings,

[1] Sayings on swearing were popular in Jewish Christianity, cf. Jas. v. 12 (for this as an anti-Pauline utterance, cf. my *St Paul and the Church of Jerusalem*, p. 338, n. 8). Disapproval of swearing is of course to be found in the rabbis (cf. Str.-B. *ad loc.*). Philo, *de Decal.* 82 ff., deprecates the use of oaths on the ground that a rational being should be so taught to speak the truth that all his words should be regarded as oaths; cf. *De Spec. Legg.* II, 2 ff. Philo here seems to be introducing a Greek conception into his treatment of the Decalogue, since such thoughts go back to the classical period, cf. Alexis quoted by Stobaeus, *Anth.* III, 27, 3 (Hense, III, 611): ὅρκος βέβαιός ἐστιν, ἂν νεύσω μόνον and the story of Diog. Laert. IV, 7 that the Athenians allowed Xenocrates to give evidence without swearing, though it was illegal for any one to do so; cf. Cicero, *Pro Balbo*, V and Val. Max. II, 10, showing that the story was a regular commonplace. According to Stobaeus, *Anth.* III, 1, 172 (Hense, III, 114), Demetrius of Phalerum in his 'Sayings of the Seven Sages' ascribed to Solon the saying φύλασσε τρόπου καλοκἀγαθίαν ὅρκου πιστοτέραν. It is possible that this line of thought came to the rabbis from Greek philosophy through the Alexandrine synagogue (note that *De Decal.* represents an older state of the halakha on oaths than Philo; cf. *Hellenistic Elements*, p. 50). It is possible that Jesus was acquainted with rabbinical views of the same kind as those quoted by Str.-B.

[2] Cf. Daube in *J.T.S.* XLV (1944), pp. 177 ff.

which reflects Jewish dislike for publicans and Gentiles which is quite out of harmony with the general attitude of Jesus.[1] The source of this and similar anti-Gentile sayings will be considered later (pp. 33 ff.).

Up to this point Matthew's version of the new Torah consists in part of a triad of sayings on three commandments of the Decalogue, drawn from a separate source, in part of elements drawn from other sources common to him and Luke, in part from yet another source peculiar to himself, replacing the original sayings on loving your enemies which lie behind Luke. Matthew, by representing the sayings on retaliation and loving your enemies as new Torah, has enhanced the difference between the new and the old, at the cost of a certain amount of misrepresentation of the best elements of rabbinical morality, which would have agreed entirely with the sayings of Jesus on these points. For whereas the original triad are a revision of the Decalogue, the last two are a correction of tolerated practice rather than of commandments or ideals; it is difficult to acquit Matthew here of a certain desire to exaggerate the extent to which the teaching of Jesus was a complete innovation. But his 'new Torah' consists of five revisions of the Decalogue and so corresponds to the five books of the old Torah, as against an original triad.

The new Torah then proceeds to a further triad of sayings, Matt. vi. 2 ff., 5 ff., and 16 ff., on the practical exercise of the new righteousness in the form of almsgiving, fasting and prayer. The triadic arrangement and the fact that the sayings are peculiar to Matthew make it possible to hold with confidence that they are drawn from the same compilation as the new Torah in its original form. They are constructed on the same pattern, with the general introduction at vi. 1: 'When you . . . , do not be as the hypocrites, for they . . . , verily I say unto you they have their reward. But when you . . . , and your father which seeth in secret shall reward you.' Again Matthew has expanded his source, adding at vi. 7 a saying from his anti-Gentile collection, and following it with the Lord's Prayer, derived

---

[1] Matthew's connecting of 'becoming sons of your Father' with the ensuing sayings reflecting a distant attitude towards the publicans and Gentiles is reminiscent of Ps. Sol. xvii. 28 f. γνώσεται γὰρ αὐτοὺς ὅτι πάντες υἱοὶ θεοῦ εἰσιν αὐτῶν, . . . καὶ πάροικος καὶ ἀλλογενὴς οὐ παροικήσει αὐτοῖς ἔτι.

from current liturgical tradition and practice,[1] and a saying on forgiveness which appears also in Mark (xi. 25). This saying is of interest since it is cast in a parallel form which is far more original, the Marcan being distinctly weaker (Mark xi. 26 appears explicable as assimilation to Matthew: it is omitted by אBWsyr.sin. and the Egyptian versions); it would thus seem that here Matthew had access to a tradition which preserved a more original form than Mark, who has it as an unattached saying on prayer in the assortment of such sayings which he has appended to the story of the barren fig tree. The remaining two sayings preserve their original form, except in so far as we may suspect that Matt. vi. 5 in the first instance ran: 'When ye pray, stand not praying in the synagogues and in the corner of the streets as the hypocrites do.'

We thus have a source with two well marked triads in parallel form. A document of this kind would be easy for a teacher and a convert to remember, and would be a natural form for a catechetical tract to take. We should indeed expect a third triad, but if there was one (and it is difficult to suppose that there was not) Matthew has omitted it, or inserted it elsewhere. The three sayings which follow

[1] For the variations between the Matthean and Lucan texts of the Lord's Prayer, cf. Creed on Luke xi. 2 ff. The position in which it appears in Luke seems to show that it is one of a miscellaneous collection of sayings and incidents put between the two tracts of the mission of the Seventy and the Beelzebub controversy; the introduction on Luke xi. 1 looks quite artificial. Hence there is no necessary reason to suppose that Matthew and Luke derive it from the same source; since the manuscript evidence for the omission of 'Thy will be done, as in heaven, so on earth' and 'But deliver us from evil' in Luke is strong while the tendency to assimilation would be overwhelming, we have every reason to suppose that Matthew and Luke are here independent. Streeter (*The Four Gospels*, p. 276) defends Marcion's reading ἐλθάτω τὸ ἅγιον πνεῦμά σου ἐφ᾽ ἡμᾶς καὶ καθαρισάτω ἡμᾶς (Marcion ap. Tert. *adv. Marc.* IV, 26 as the first petition; in 700, 162, Greg. Nyss., Max., as the second); this view is rightly rejected by Creed *ad loc*. It may be added to his arguments that καθαρίζειν in early New Testament literature is always used in a more or less definitely ritual sense, either of Jewish cleansings (e.g. Mark i. 40 ff. and parallels) or of declaring 'clean' what the Torah regards as 'unclean' (Acts x. 15, where the source is early) or of the real 'cleansings' of Judaism (Acts xv. 9). In II Cor. vii. 1 it is used of cleansing ourselves by coming out from among unbelievers in reference to Isa. lii. 11, in Eph. vi. 26 of baptism. The nearest approach to the purely spiritual sense implied in the Marcionite version is I John i. 9; but cf. 7 where cleansing by the blood of Jesus puts us into the sphere of associations of Old Testament ritual and the sacrament of Baptism. It does not appear to be used in a purely ethical sense where no reference to ceremonial purification or 'cleansing' by a process in some sense analogous to such purification is provided by the context.

(Matt. vi. 19–24) consist of matter also found in various contexts in Luke and have no claim to be considered as part of such a document, since they consist of general ethical maxims, and have no common structure; they have a common subject, since all deal with the right to wealth, but in a general way and without reference to special laws or special duties.[1] Moreover the first (Matt. vi. 19–21) has more claim to stand in its Lucan position. It concludes the discourse on wealth in Luke xii. 22–34, and Matthew has detached it from that place in order to provide a transition from his triadic source to the Lucan sermon on wealth. It is none the less probable that Matthew has preserved the more primitive form of the saying; the parallelism of the structure and the picturesque detail look original, while Luke gives a rather colourless summary.[2] There is little verbal similarity

[1] For triads in Jewish teaching cf. *Pirke Aboth* ii. 1, 10–14; iii, 1; v. 22. It is conceivable that the tract contained two triads with an introduction forming a hebdomad, but this seems less likely. For the triad in popular teaching cf. B. T. D. Smith, *Parables of the Synoptic Gospels*, p. 35. It is possible that the three parables of the kingdom in xiii. 44 ff. formed the original completion of this source, the theme of the kingdom of heaven bringing us back to the opening theme of v. 20; they offer an invitation to the kingdom and a warning to the unworthy. The conclusion (xiii. 51 f.) would suit the proclamation of the new Torah; does it express the same anti-Paulinism as v. 17 ff.? If so, the whole section v. 17–20 may have formed the introduction to the new Torah in Matthew's source, and its compilation will be the work of a predecessor. But see below, p. 35.

[2] Kilpatrick, *Origins*, p. 75, regards Matthew's form as a liturgical expansion, into which Matthew has introduced his 'favourite' antithesis of heaven and earth, as well as the parallelism of form. But it seems very doubtful whether he is right in regarding the antithesis of heaven and earth as a favourite of Matthew. It is true that he uses it thirteen times, as against Luke's five and Mark's two. But five of these occur in the passage Matt. xviii. 18 f. and the doublet of xviii. 18 in xvi. 19; xviii. 18 seems to be the original version, and with xviii. 19 to come from a fragment of a very ancient Jewish-Christian 'Church-order' (see below, p. 133). It is hard to see how the thought could be expressed otherwise; in any event Matthew is following his source, and there is no reason to suppose that he has edited it in this respect. Matt. xxiv. 35 is taken over from Mark xiii. 31; it is to be noticed that at xxiv. 31 the antithesis of Mark xiii. 27 has been changed by Matthew into 'from one end of the heaven to the other'. Matt. v. 18 is from the Q stratum (=Luke xvi. 17) as is Matt. xi. 25=Luke x. 21; here Pap. 45 and Marcion omit καὶ τῆς γῆς, but in view of the almost complete verbal identity of the whole passage Matt. xi. 25–7 and Luke x. 22 f. it is very doubtful if the omission can be justified. This leaves five cases peculiar to Matthew, of which vi. 10, in the Lord's Prayer, is hardly likely to come from Matthew's editing; so venerable a formula would hardly be altered deliberately by the evangelist on his own authority, and the change probably represents the formula as used in the Church for which Matthew writes. Matt. v. 34 f. and xxiii. 9 may be due to Matthew, but they may equally well be due to his sources. The antithesis of heaven and earth

except in the concluding words; their epigrammatic character has here, as often, preserved a verbal identity for a particular saying while the general body of sayings has been largely altered. The second (Matt. vi. 22–3) appears in Luke as a floating saying in the section xi. 33–6 which has no continuity with the preceding or following sections; it is to be presumed that it had no established position in the tradition, and that Luke put it in at a point between two different sections because he knew of no better place; this implies that its position in Matthew is also the work of the evangelist. In neither case have we a real context; as Luke xi. 34 stands, the meaning seems to be that 'as the light of the body depends on the eye, so, it is implied, does the light of man's life depend on his heart', while Luke xi. 36 as it stands gives 'an intolerably platitudinous meaning', perhaps the consequence of a primitive corruption (so Creed *ad loc.*). Matthew found the words in the source which he shares with Luke; the sayings on the lamp of the body are very nearly identical as far as Matt. vi. 22 f. and Luke xi. 34 f. are concerned; Matthew has either corrected the Lucan platitude or preserved the original sense underlying the Lucan corruption. Matthew has, however, narrowed the Lucan meaning by substituting for the general state of man's heart his attitude to riches.[1]

On the other hand the third saying on serving two masters (vi. 24) formed the original opening to the Q discourse (Matt. vi. 25–34= Luke xii. 22–31) on the right attitude to wealth which Matthew puts immediately after it. Luke opens his discourse with the quite impossible formula 'And he said unto his disciples, Therefore I say unto you'. 'And he said unto them' implies the opening of a new

---

is a regular Old Testament usage; and it may well be the case that the Jewish-Christian sources used by Matthew are faithful in this respect to the actual usage of Jesus; his alteration of Mark xiii. 37 into another Old Testament phrase (Deut. xxx. 4) does not suggest a special predilection for the antithesis.

[1] Str.-B. on Matt. vi. 22 may be right in holding that the original saying had no special reference to liberality or stinginess. (For this sense of 'single' cf. their parallels on Matt. xx. 15.) But the association of the 'good' and 'evil' eye with liberality and stinginess was so strong that Matthew thought it natural to transfer them to their present position, where they describe not generosity in giving but lack of undue concern for riches which is necessary for any genuine liberality. It is certainly possible that the words originally referred to giving and the right attitude to wealth and had lost this specific meaning before they reached the common source; if so Matthew has rightly restored the original meaning.

saying or group of sayings in a series where each saying or group is a separate unit as in the Oxyrhynchus Logia; 'Therefore I say unto you' implies that the collection of sayings has already been compiled into a continuous discourse so that the formula introduces a saying which is ostensibly a logical inference from the preceding one. On the other hand the saying on serving two masters has no claim to its present Lucan position at Luke xvi. 13; it is merely inserted there to counteract the unfortunate impression which might be produced by the parable of the unjust steward when its original meaning had been lost (cf. below, pp. 93 ff.); and the transference would be the easier in view of the position of the parable of the rich fool in Luke xii. 16–21. It would seem that Luke had before him a discourse on riches, which opened with the words: 'And he said unto his disciples "No man can serve two masters . . . ye cannot serve God and Mammon. Therefore I say unto you . . ." ' with the rest of xii. 22–34. Luke removed 'No man . . . God and Mammon' but carelessly left in 'Therefore I say unto you'. Matthew has inserted the whole collection including the two masters (the wording in both Gospels is practically identical including the striking verbs μισήσει . . . ἀγαπήσει . . . ἀνθέξεται . . . καταφρονήσει), and again carelessly pre-served at vi. 25 the 'Therefore I say unto you', which is quite out of keeping with the general style of his Sermon which proceeds from point to point in a series of commandments, not linked together by any formula of this kind. (His only similar introduction of a logical connexion in the Sermon on the Mount is the quite colourless 'there-fore' at vii. 12 and 24.)

The discourse on worldly riches is practically identical in both evangelists apart from Luke's introduction of a more general word-ing at xii. 26 to enforce his point and his similar introduction of μὴ μετεωρίζεσθε at xii. 29, and Matthew's insertion of the striking sayings of vi. 34 from a separate source; otherwise there seems no reason that might account for its omission by Luke.[1]

---

[1] Possibly Matthew found it in his anti-Gentile source. Admittedly this is only guesswork, but it is conceivable that it was used as an anti-Pauline argument, reminiscent of Jas. iv. 13; cf. *St Paul and the Church of Jerusalem*, p. 338, n. 8, on II Cor. i. 15 ff. And there is in any event no reason to suppose that all the matter in the source had been so coloured by the document's main tendency as to make the anti-Gentile character unambiguous throughout. In all probability it also contained 'neutral' material.

At this point Matthew returns to the Sermon as he found it in the common source, and inserts the sayings (Matt. vii. 1–5) on not judging others with the changes already noticed (p. 15); the matter which he has retained shows an almost complete verbal identity with Luke.[1] He appends a saying (from his anti-Gentile source?) on casting pearls before swine (vii. 6), which seems to have no relevance to the context, unless it is intended to counteract the danger that the saying as to not judging others might be interpreted as condemning the Jew who judged the Gentile on the lines of Rom. ii. 1. If this view be correct, we have here a survival of a very early controversy.[2] At this point it would seem that Matthew found that while he had inserted the Lord's Prayer, the rest of the tract on prayer common to him and Luke (xi. 1–13; see below, p. 60) was left on his hands. Having decided to omit the parable of Luke xi. 5–8 (perhaps because it added nothing to the teaching which followed) he added here the remainder (Matt. vii. 7–11 = Luke xi. 9–13) and so cleared it out of his way, although it rather spoils the general symmetry of the Sermon.[3] This is followed by the Golden Rule (vii. 12) transferred

[1] The saying 'With what measure ye mete' is proverbial (cf. Str.-B. on Matt. vii. 2); it appears at Mark iv. 24 where it is followed by 'and it shall be added unto you', meaning apparently 'as you do towards God, so and more will He do to you'. This is followed in the next verse by the saying 'He that hath, to him shall be given', which also appears in the Lucan parallel (viii. 18), while Matthew transfers it to the opening of the explanation of the use of parables (xiii. 12). But it also appears in the parable of the pounds in Luke xix. 26 (= the talents, Matt. xxv. 29). The Marcan context looks like a collection of isolated sayings. In Matthew its appearance as a conclusion to the parable of the talents is effective and appropriate; the Lucan version of the pounds has been altered considerably (cf. Creed ad loc.), while the introduction of xix. 25 gives a hopelessly awkward arrangement (Creed regards it as an early insertion in view of the textual authority for its omission). It seems likely that both sayings are rightly placed in Luke vi. 37 (= Matt. vii. 2) and xix. 26 (= Matt. xxv. 29), while Mark only knew these as isolated sayings.

[2] But it may, like the section which follows, have stood in a source (or section of a source) which he wished to finish off and have done with. It is of course possible that Jesus at some time warned his followers against indiscreet teaching of unsuitable hearers. But the saying, to which there are many parallels (cf. Str.-B. and Wetstein ad loc.), is more violent than any recorded, though quite in keeping with the tone of the anti-Gentile source.

[3] Luke's wording may be original in so far as it differs from Matthew. The grotesque 'scorpion' instead of an egg seems to have been softened down by Matthew into a stone instead of bread. Against this, however, must be weighed the fact that 'a scorpion instead of a perch' was a familiar Greek proverb which appears in the collections of Hadrianic date by Zenobius (1, 88, Leutsch-Schneidewin, *Paroemio-*

from its early Lucan position in order to mark the end of the Torah of the Kingdom of Heaven, as expanded from the conflation of the Sermon with the triadic 'new Torah'; here it provides an excellent end to the Torah proper, corresponding to its beginning in v. 17. The saying in its Matthean form has been expanded by the addition of the Law and the prophets to secure this correspondence.

The new Torah proper is then enforced by a series of warnings (Matt. vii. 13 ff.); it is probable that Matthew had in mind the warnings and promises with which Leviticus and Deuteronomy conclude their versions of the Torah (Lev. xxvi. 3–end, Deut. xxviii–xxx). For this purpose he detaches from their original position the sayings on the narrow gate, which in Luke appear in the collection of sayings xiii. 22 ff., which appears to be a Lucan compilation of unattached material (see below, pp. 78 ff.). It is possible that Matthew has preserved the original form while Luke has abbreviated, perhaps from failure to appreciate the Semitic parallelism, but it is perhaps more probable that Matthew had a somewhat different version of the sayings from Luke; the only identical words are στενή and πολλοί. To the warning on entering in by the narrow gate Matthew adds the section from the sermon on trees and their fruits from the Q Sermon. But it serves an entirely different purpose, since it is a warning against false prophets. Here we are in an atmosphere of apocalypse, which reflects the state of Palestine and the primitive Jewish Church in the years preceding the rebellion as in Mark xiii. 6 ff.; we are coming to the last day at vii. 22 and the false prophets who are to precede it are appropriate at this point. But the general ethical teaching of the Lucan form is no doubt the original sense.

The section on hearing and doing (Matt. vii. 21–3 = Luke vi. 46

---

graphi Graeci, i, p. 29) and Diogenianus (i, 76, p. 193), and so passes into the later Byzantine collections of Gregory of Cyprus (i, 53, p. 354), Apostolius (iii, 7, *ib.* ii, p. 289), and the Lexicon of 'Suidas', s.v. ἀντὶ πέρκης σκορπίον. The proverb may have been known to Luke and so led him to substitute his wording for an original 'stone for bread'. It is difficult to decide which view is the more probable. At Luke xi. 11, however, the unusual phrase πνεῦμα ἀγαθόν (𝔓 45, a few Greek MSS. and the Vulgate) looks more original and has led to the confused variants ἀγαθὸν δόμα D old Latin, δόματα ἀγαθά Θ, πνεῦμα ἅγιον being the reading that achieved most currency. The phrase πνεῦμα ἀγαθόν is not common, but appears in Neh. ix, 20 LXX and in *Test. XII Patr. Benj.* iv, 5 (though here with a textual variant). It could hardly fail to be emended by any well intentioned scribe.

and xiii. 26 f.) shows a remarkable variation. Matthew's fuller form of the opening words gives a regular Semitic parallelism which has every claim to be regarded as original. It may have been abbreviated by Luke in his Sermon; we have seen that he frequently fails to reproduce these parallelisms. Possibly the longer form came to Matthew as a floating tradition, or from one of his other sources; but Luke may simply be abbreviating. In the verses that follow Matthew is still altering a general warning of urgency into a specific warning against false prophets, since they dominate his scene from vii. 13–23. Consequently the social intercourse of the Lucan version becomes the false working of miracles in Matthew. It is possible but not probable that Luke has altered the saying that follows (xiii. 28) from a warning to disciples in general into a warning to the Jews (cf. Creed *ad loc.*). On the other hand the 'master of the house' in Luke xiii. 25, who answers those cast out in xiii. 27, is original as against the 'I' of Matthew, which reflects a developed Christology; yet again, the parallelism and the interrogative form of Matthew seem to belong to the original, which may have run: 'Did we not eat before thee and did we not drink before thee and did we not stand before thee when thou taughtest in our streets?' The section ends with the quotation from Ps. vi. 9, in which the first four words agree with the LXX of Swete's edition (i.e. Codex B), while the last four of Matthew agree with the LXX as against Luke. It would seem that the evangelists give the Greek text as known to them from different versions of the Greek Bible and that neither version corresponded exactly with the LXX of the great uncial manuscripts.

The Sermon ends with the parable of the two houses; here again Luke has spoiled the Semitic parallelism of Matt. vii. 24 ff. (=Luke vi. 47 ff.). This he has largely done by substituting a syntactic construction for the parataxis of Matthew, a clear sign that his version here is secondary as against Matthew's. The loss of parallelism is also partly due to his substitution of a fine Hellenistic house with foundations for the peasant's hut of Matthew (cf. Smith, p. 225). Clearly here Matthew's version is nearer the original, a point which is of some importance in showing that Matthew's parallelism is, at least in some cases, original and not editorial (cf. above, p. 16, n. 1). One further element in Matthew's Sermon remains to be considered. It has been noticed above (p. 25) that we have several scattered sayings which reflect a bitter hostility to Gentiles as such. Two of these occur in the Sermon on the Mount (Matt. v. 47 and vi. 7), the third at Matt. xviii. 17; in the first and third, Gentiles are coupled with publicans. In each case the Gentiles are referred to as ἐθνικοί, a term which seems to carry with it a suggestion of contempt as in Gal. ii. 14, where Paul's use of the adverb expresses the contempt of the Pharisee for the Jew who lives no better than the Gentile.[1] In any case in these passages there is a definite tone of hostility, the Gentile being equated with the heathen and the publican, not simply as a technical term for one who is not a Jew (or a Christian).

The attitude of contemptuous hostility to Gentiles and publicans is entirely contrary to the general Synoptic tradition including that of Matthew himself; cf. xi. 19 and xxi. 31, peculiar to him, for publicans; for Gentiles cf. xxviii. 19 which we may with some confidence ascribe to Matthew himself, and the emphasis placed on the Q saying (Luke xiii. 28 f.) by its insertion at Matt. viii. 11 f. in the story of the centurion's servant, to show that the Gentiles are eligible for the kingdom no less than the Jews.

This attitude is again different from that of Matt. v. 20 and xiii. 52 if the interpretation suggested for these passages above (p. 20) is correct. Gentile converts of Paul are 'in' the kingdom of heaven; it is probable that Matthew thought that Gentile converts should enter the Church as proselytes, but there is no doubt that he, and the Church he writes for, accepted them.[2]

The extent of this source or stratum cannot be judged. It may have included the whole of the Matthean version of the Q version

---

[1] The word also occurs at III John 7 with no such suggestion; some MSS. read ἐθνῶν but the ἐθνικῶν of ℵ, A, B, C and D is clearly to be preferred, since the change of ἐθνικῶν to the commoner ἐθνῶν is far more likely than the reverse. But III John is late enough for the writer to have taken over the word from the Synoptic tradition, if not from one of our Gospels (cf. Dodd, *The Johannine Epistles*, Moffatt Commentary, pp. xxviii ff.), and he seems to use the word simply in the sense of ἐθνῶν. If in fact the word is used with this tone of hostility, it would seem to be a peculiarity of Palestinian Greek.

For the use of the word cf. K. L. Schmidt in *T.W.z.N.T.* s.v. ἔθνος. He does not note the fact that ἐθνικός is only used with this tone of hostility, except for III John 7. Kilpatrick, *Origins*, p. 117, rightly recognizes the 'derogatory suggestion'.

[2] Cf. Kilpatrick, *Origins*, pp. 108 and 117 ff.

of the Sermon in Matt. v. 38–48 (=Luke vi. 27–36) and perhaps more of the Sermon, as found in both evangelists, since it no doubt also included sayings without a definitely anti-Gentile character (above, p. 29, n. 1). There is no measure of verbal identity which compels us to suppose that they are both using an identical document rather than two versions of an archetype which has been considerably modified in details of order and wording in the course of its earlier transmission. On the other hand it does not appear to have included the original triads on the revised Decalogue and prayer, fasting and almsgiving, since vi. 7 is a Matthean addition to the original structure in which each of the second group of triads has a fixed ending. It may have included the whole of the fragmentary 'Church order' of xviii. 15–20,[1] and probably vii. 6 is drawn from it as well.[2] It is possible that we owe to it the preservation of what appears to be the original form of the non-Marcan charge to the Twelve, where such verses as x. 5 f. and 23 are to be regarded not as later Jewish-Christian additions but as the preservation of an original charge, which has been used as a series of 'proof-texts' to condemn missions to the Gentiles (cf. below, pp. 49 f.). It may also be the source of the peculiar features of Matthew's version of the story of the Syrophoenician woman (xv. 21 ff.; cf. Vol. 1, p. 54).

In any event it would seem that we have here a stratum of tradition which has been coloured by the communal quarrels of Jews and Gentiles in the cities on the fringes of Judaea proper.[3] No doubt in such circles Gentile converts would have been admitted if they came as proselytes of Judaism, but it is unlikely that they would be encouraged.[4] It is not in the least surprising that Matthew, if he

---

[1] Professor Dodd suggests (*New Testament Studies*, 1953, pp. 57–8) that 'the Church' of xviii. 17 is the Church of Jerusalem, and that the passage goes back to a period when the only organized Church was that of Jerusalem and the immediate neighbourhood. If so, the source is of very high antiquity.

[2] For 'swine' as a description of Gentiles, cf. Str.-B. *ad loc.* For 'dogs' in the same sense *idem*, 1, 724 f.

[3] Cf. Josephus, *B.J.* 11, 284 ff. and 559; note especially 461. Agabus in Acts xxi. 10 appears to be on quite good terms with the Gentile Christians of Caesarea. But the tradition of hatred shown in this stratum might easily have existed at some less important centre, where the Christians were strict in their Judaism and there were no Gentile converts.

[4] It is instructive to compare the different views as to proselytes expressed by rabbinical writers; cf. Moore, *Judaism*, 1, 338 ff.

found what he regarded as a valuable source, should include it
bodily in spite of the fact that it did not agree with his own outlook;
this was a common practice of Hellenistic compilers and examples
could be multiplied from the later ecclesiastical historians. It is quite
natural that such circles might retain very good traditions of the
actual teaching of Jesus which, through slight modifications, might
be given a marked anti-Gentile bias. Thus the reference to
βατταλογία is probably not to be taken as referring to the heathen
and Jewish practice of heaping up names and epithets to enforce an
answer to prayer[1] in contrast to the simplicity of the Lord's Prayer
(which may not be drawn from the same source). It seems more
likely that it refers to the incoherent and sometimes inarticulate
prayers of the type described by Apuleius in his account of the
votaries of the Syrian goddess; prayers of this kind seem characteristic of Syrian religion, and would naturally be regarded as characteristic of Gentiles as such by their Jewish neighbours on the borders
of Palestine.[2]

It must, however, be recognized that it is impossible to be sure
whether we have here a source of a documentary character or simply
some scattered fragments of oral tradition. It would be tempting
to see in Matt. xviii. 15–17 the third triad of the source which provided Matthew with his revision of the Decalogue and the rules of
prayer, fasting and almsgiving. But against this it must be observed
that the reference to Gentile methods of prayer is not part of the
original teaching on prayer, as was noted above. It would be quite
possible that v. 17 was added to an older pre-Matthean collection of
sayings in the anti-Gentile circle we have been considering, and that
the same circle has coloured the 'Church order' of xviii. 15 ff. with
its peculiar slant; but this is purely conjectural.

On any showing the Matthean Sermon is a highly composite
document. It is based on the Lucan Sermon as found in Q with the
Beatitudes drawn from a different version. This has been amplified
by the insertion of the new Torah (which has been amplified and
structurally spoilt by the Matthean additions, especially Matt. v. 38
and 43 which represent the matter drawn from the Q Sermon as
revisions of the Torah when in fact it is nothing of the kind),

[1] So Delling in *T.W.z.N.T.* s.v.
[2] Apuleius, *Metam.* VIII, 7, 582; cf. I Kings xviii. 26.

and the triad on prayer, fasting and almsgiving. This is followed by matter drawn from various parts of the Q stratum as found in various parts of Luke. At various points he has either introduced matter from his anti-Gentile tradition, or, perhaps more probably, has used material which had passed through anti-Gentile circles and been coloured by their peculiar views. As a literary structure it cannot be said that the Sermon deserves the praise often bestowed on it; from vi. 12 to vii. 11 it is peculiarly chaotic.

The Sermon is in no sense a masterpiece of rhetorical artistry. For the most part Matthew's share in it consists not in skilful arrangement but in the mechanical aggregation of the material which came to him. The natural explanation of the place which the Sermon has always held in the life of Christian devotion is that apart from a few additions it is made up of the words of Jesus himself.

PART II
THE SOURCES OF LUKE

CHAPTER III

THE INFANCY NARRATIVE

Luke opens his Gospel with a preface on the best classical lines, pointing out that while many have preceded him in writing a history of the facts on which the Church's message is founded, no one has such good qualifications as he has in view of his acquaintance with the original eye-witnesses and his care for scrupulous accuracy.[1] He does not, as is usual, emphasize the importance of his subject, but it is taken for granted that Theophilus, as an instructed Christian, recognizes this. It may be noted in his favour that he states his claims in four verses, while his contemporaries allow themselves several chapters. His claim to have 'kept in touch' with the facts by personal investigation (cf. Creed, *ad loc.*) must not be pressed too closely; it was customary for the Hellenistic historian to cut up the works of his predecessors and then to claim that he had travelled far and wide to visit the scenes of the events he records and consulted the official public records, the eye-witnesses and so on (cf. Diod. Sic. 1, 4, 1 ff.).

From this typical Hellenistic prologue, written in the best Greek of which he is capable, Luke plunges into his story of the Birth of Jesus. It has been suggested that it is his own composition in style deliberately imitated from the LXX;[2] the suggestion is sometimes so stated as to arouse suspicion that the view is based more on the desire

---

[1] Thucydides appears to be the first extant representative of the tradition with his claim that from the outset he foresaw the importance of the Peloponnesian war and began to write a history of it. In length Josephus, *B.J.* 1, 1, is comparable to Thucydides, from whom he has borrowed unblushingly the claim that the Jewish war was almost the greatest in history. He is severe on the motives and veracity of his predecessors. Polybius on the other hand does not give his name or qualifications, but deals with the greatness of his theme and his 'philosophy of history'. It is the combination of the two types which produces the portentous introductions of Diodorus Siculus; Dionysius of Halicarnassus is even worse, but his task is complicated by the necessity of proving to the Greek world that it was mistaken in regarding the Romans as barbarians; he does not really come to his own qualifications till c. 7, where at least he is honest enough to admit that he derives most of his information from literary sources.

[2] This is argued by Harnack, *Sitzungsber. d. preuss. Akad.* (1900), pp. 538 ff.; *Luke the Physician* (1907), pp. 199–218.

to find a short cut for getting rid of the doctrine of the Virgin Birth[1] than on a serious study of the Greek in which the story is written. On the whole it presents an orgy of Hebraic Greek with occasional improvements; it is of course possible to argue that we have an attempt by Luke to imitate Hebraic Greek on the strength of his knowledge of the LXX, and that his occasional 'improvements' are simply lapses from his general attempt to produce an imitation of Hebrew, but here the argument will not really meet the facts; the only explanation of them seems to be that he attempted to bring his source into some sort of tolerable Greek but abandoned the attempt.[2] Moreover, ὕψιστος is treated as a proper name without the article; in all three cases where it is used it appears as a subjective genitive and in all three cases the noun which governs it has no article before it. This is of course the normal Hebrew usage; but it is not the normal usage of the LXX. It appears to represent a relatively late change of practice, ὕψιστος being regarded as a name, not as a description, the reason for the change being that as a description it might be taken to imply that there are others who are gods, even if they are not so exalted as the Most Highest (cf. Philo, *Leg. Alleg.* III, 8). The fact that Luke consistently follows the late LXX usage suggests that he is reproducing the usage of a source which was consistent in doing so.[3]

[1] Cf. *Hellenistic Elements*, pp. 22–5.

[2] It is noticeable that in i. 6 we have ταῖς ἐντολαῖς τοῦ κυρίου and in i. 9 τὸν ναὸν τοῦ κυρίου. Elsewhere κύριος is treated normally as a proper name and we find, as in the LXX, a completely chaotic variation in the use of the article, with a noun followed by κύριος as a subjective genitive; thus in i. 30 (ἡ δούλη κυρίου) and in ii. 22–4. On the other hand we have ἄγγελος κυρίου in i. 11 and 29 and χεὶρ κυρίου in i. 66. Here we may have the influence of Christian Greek; cf. below, p. 125, and Acts v. 19, viii. 26, xii. 7 and 23 (all in the first half of Acts) and xi. 21 and xiii. 11 for χεὶρ κυρίου, the latter being in *oratio recta* in the mouth of Paul, though it is more likely simply due to the influence of Christian Greek than to a deliberate attempt by Luke to put Semitic Greek into Paul's words. Again while κύριος is usually a proper name as in the LXX we have the article before it in i. 46 and ii. 22, just as we have it occasionally, at any rate in the oblique cases, in the LXX. For a good specimen of the sort of confusion we find in Hebraic Greek cf. *Ps. Sol.* ii. 36. The correct Greek usage in i. 6 and 9, which is the rarest in the LXX, is easily understood as an attempt by Luke to correct the usage of his source, abandoned in view of the difficulty of the task; it is hard to suppose that he would have used it if he was trying to imitate the LXX.

[3] The normal LXX usage is to use the article before ὕψιστος and where it is used as a subjective genitive to put the article before the noun on which it depends,

Concerning the problem of the origins of this source the most attractive solution is perhaps that offered by H. L. MacNeill,[1] who sees in these chapters a first attempt to link together the movement started by John the Baptist with a primitive Jewish Christianity somewhere between A.D. 30 and 70. There are certain of his assumptions with which I should wish to quarrel; for instance, 'the prevailing view' that there was once a large Baptist movement, which came to be steadily overshadowed by the growth of Christianity, rests on what seems to me extremely slender evidence. Once it is recognized that the Mandeans' claim to be descended from the original followers of John probably represents no more than their anxiety to prove themselves 'a people of the Book' in the days of

although this is not in accordance with Hebrew usage. The use of the article is the more striking since in the Hebrew *Elioun* has no article. Cf. Ezra viii. 19, Pss. xii. 13, xxi. 7, lxxvii. 10, cvii. 11. Ps. lxxxii. 6 is an exception, since while υἱοί does not demand the article there is none before ὑψίστου, as there is at xci. 1 where again the article is not needed before βοήθεια and appears before ὑψίστου. Num. xxiv. 16 appears to be the only exception till we come to Lam. iii. 35 and 38; in Dan. vii. 18 LXX and Theodotion we find ἅγιοι ὑψίστου but in 22 the LXX has τοῖς ... τοῦ ... while Theodotion has ἁγίοις ὑψίστου in 25. Daniel has the correct Greek, while Theodotion has τοῖς ἁγίοις ὑψίστου. In Wisd. v. 15 and vi. 3 ὕψιστος appears without the article. In Ecclesiasticus the title is used forty-seven times, five times with the article in the nominative (but two are doubtful readings); in xxxiii. 15 we have τὰ ἔργα τοῦ ὑψίστου; in xxiii. 9 we have ὀνομασίᾳ τοῦ ὑψίστου, but it is a v.l. and I should be inclined to suspect xxxiii. 15. Elsewhere the title is used without the article and where it is a subjective genitive the main noun has no article either (e.g. xix. 17, xxiv. 2, 3 and 23).

It looks as though the usage of Ecclesiasticus represents a late stratum of Old Testament Greek, which has perhaps infiltrated from the Greek synagogue into Palestinian usage. In any event it seems most unlikely that Luke, if trying to compose a Hebraic Greek document, would have followed the usage of Ecclesiasticus as against the general Old Testament practice. He has indeed υἱοὶ ὑψίστου in vi. 35, but here he is presumably following his source which Matthew has altered (v. 35). Elsewhere (viii. 28, Acts vii. 48 and xvi. 17) the title is treated as adjectival.

It is curious that Luke i. 17 is very much nearer to Ecclus. xlviii. 10 than to Mal. iv. 5; in Luke and Ecclesiasticus we have ἐπίστρεψαι instead of ἀποκαταστῆσαι, while in Ecclesiasticus it is to be Elijah's function καταστῆσαι φύλας Ἰακώβ which appears to be represented by Luke's ἑτοιμάσαι κυρίῳ λαὸν κατεσκευασμένον (on which cf. Creed *ad loc.*). Malachi has nothing to correspond. I can only suppose that this interpretation of Malachi was current in Jewish circles which were looking for the Consolation. καταστῆσαι seems difficult as equivalent to ἀποκαταστῆσαι, but in Isa. xlix 8 appears to mean 'bring to order', which is perhaps the sense in Ecclus. xlviii. 10.

[1] 'The Sitz im Leben of Luke i. 5–ii. 20', in *Journal of Biblical Literature*, LXV (1946), pp. 123–30.

the Mohammedan conquests,[1] our knowledge of such a movement is confined to the story of Apollos and the twelve disciples of John who appear at Ephesus in Acts xix. 1 ff.

Again, I cannot really attach any meaning to the statement that a local corporate group is responsible for these chapters rather than an individual. Such language is frequently used, but that does not make it more meaningful. A story must originate with a story-teller, though no doubt it depends upon his hearers whether the story meets with such approval that in consequence it is preserved. A conflation of the birth stories of John and Jesus might be the work of some committee appointed to unite them. But the Lucan story hardly reads like the work of a committee. No doubt it emanates from someone who could gauge the feelings of his hearers and their readiness to accept his narrative; and the way may have been prepared for him by earlier story-tellers in the same milieu.

Nor can I see any justification for MacNeill's assumption that the story of the Virgin Birth, i.e. Luke i. 34–7, is a later insertion, the dominant thought in the section i. 26–56 being not the Virgin Birth so much as the Messiahship of Jesus. There seems no reason for this view apart from the modern difficulty of belief in the historicity of the Virgin Birth. But the story as it stands demands that the miracle of the birth of the Baptist from parents who are too old to have a child should be paralleled and surpassed by an even greater miracle marking the birth of Jesus. It is indeed tenable that the Virgin Birth was interpolated into an older story current among followers of Jesus, the Virgin Birth having been added when it was necessary to outbid the miraculous birth of the Baptist before the story reached Luke.[2] Unfortunately, this sacrifices the only approach to a justification for the omission of πῶς ἔσται... γινώσκω in i. 34 by the old Latin MS. b; it will hardly be urged that it had access to a pre-Lucan form of the story.

But MacNeill's suggestion that the whole narrative emanates from

[1] For the view that the Baptist is a late introduction into Mandean religion cf. Brandt in Hastings' *Encyclopaedia of Religion and Ethics*, VIII, pp. 390 ff. It would be easy and natural for the Mandeans to produce or to revise literature to make it appear that they were descended from a great prophetic figure of the Bible. (For the Mandeans see further *Gentiles*, pp. 212 ff.)

[2] Cf. the rabbinical enlargements on the miraculous birth of Isaac in Genesis Rabba on Gen. xvii. 17; xviii. 11. For the whole theory cf. Creed, pp. 13 f.

a primitive period in which Jewish Christianity was in contact with a sect of followers of the Baptist, such as may very well have existed in the hill country of Judaea,[1] has much to be said for it. It explains the Messianic character of the Baptist and the double character of the whole narrative, without needing to assume the existence of a large, coherent and influential Baptist sect, gradually eliminated by the Church, which could only be re-discovered by reading a vast amount between the lines of the New Testament, even if we are not driven to the desperate expedient of invoking the Mandeans to support the hypothesis.[2] There must have been followers of the Baptist, and it is quite probable that in the Lucan infancy narrative is preserved a memory of the absorption of what may well have been a small body of Jewish followers of the Baptist by the rising tide of Christianity.[3]

---

[1] The prominence of the ὀρεινή, the toparchy of Judaea in which Jerusalem is situated (Schürer, *Gesch. d. jüd. Volkes*, II, 230), is a striking feature of the narrative; normally in the Gospels we read of specific places, or their immediate neighbourhood, such as the borders of Tyre, Mark vii. 24, or the villages of Caesarea Philippi, Mark viii. 27, except for Decapolis in Mark viii. 31, where, however, Jesus is passing through the district on a journey. Naturally the larger districts such as Galilee and Judaea are mentioned, but otherwise events are attached to particular places. It would seem that the events were attached by tradition to the neighbourhood of Jerusalem, but could not be located in the city, except where the Temple was involved. I suspect that Luke himself felt the peculiarity and inserted the vague 'city of Judah' at i. 39.

[2] The treatment of the Baptist in Mark may of course be influenced by the desire to minimize the importance of the Baptist and his claims to be the Messiah in the interests of the Church's belief in the Messiahship of Jesus; but it is equally compatible with the view that the Baptist regarded himself from the beginning as the prophet who was to prepare the way for the Messiah. The Fourth evangelist does not mention the baptism of Jesus; his silence may of course be due either (*a*) to the desire to avoid the problem of why Jesus should be baptized at all, as in Matt. iii. 13 f.; (*b*) to the writer's general assumption that his readers know the synoptic tradition, which therefore need not be repeated; or (*c*) to mere slovenliness on his part. The treatment of the Baptist in the Fourth Gospel, while it might imply a desire to diminish his importance, might equally well be due to the necessity of proving that in the Baptist the forerunner of the Messiah, foretold by Mal. iii. 1, had really appeared. For the importance of this cf. Justin, *Dial.* 49 (268 A), and for the difficulties involved cf. Tert. *de Anima* 35, Origen, *in Ev. Jo.* VI, 10, 62 ff.

[3] I am not quite clear what MacNeill means by saying that 'there is nothing distinctively Christian in these chapters'. It is true that in these chapters Jesus is distinctly the Jewish Messiah, who is to bring the Consolation of Israel. But it is very hard to suppose that any community of this kind existed before the belief that Jesus had risen from the dead; we have no trace of any 'community' as against the Twelve and some more loosely attached followers. If, however, he means that the narrative is the work of one who regards Jesus as the Messiah who will return to earth to set

This absorption was no doubt not entirely negligible in its impact on the Christian community, as is shown not only by the Lucan infancy narrative in itself but also by the echoes of the *Benedictus* in the language of Peter in Acts iii. 19–21, where Luke i. 70 reappears almost *verbatim* with reference to the ἀποκατάστασις with its overtones reminiscent of the Elijah theme of Malachi (see above, p. 41, n.).

up the kingdom of David, he is merely saying that the writer took a rather Jewish view as to what the Second Coming would involve. Cf. the supernatural Messianic Kingdom of the descendant of David in *Ps. Sol.* xvii. 23 ff. See Moore, *Judaism*, ii. 324 ff. and, for the currency of hopes of a Messianic Kingdom on earth in primitive Christianity, Mark x. 37, Acts i. 6.

CHAPTER IV

Q TRACTS

It has already been observed that apart from the sections considered in Part I, the evidence for a single document Q as the source of all or most of the material common to Matthew and Luke is by no means conclusive. The important point, however, is to discover whether such a document, if it ever existed, can be shown to have been a compilation of shorter tracts which had an independent existence as collections of the sayings of Jesus; whether they had been joined together into a larger whole before they reached the evangelists is a secondary question. Luke's general habit of keeping his sources in their original form makes it necessary to use him as the main test for deciding the question.

Naturally it is not necessary to suppose that all Luke's material came to him in this form, or that, even if it did, we can be certain of identifying all of these tracts. The evidence suggests that he had a certain number of isolated fragments, whether of narrative or discourse, which he inserts between his other blocks of material, sometimes because they appeared to have some reference to a particular situation, sometimes for no apparent reason; they had to be inserted somewhere, and one place was as good as another.[1]

[1] Thus the Samaritan village (ix. 51 ff.) was localized at Samaria and so comes at the beginning of the journey to Jerusalem; Zacchaeus (xix. 1 ff.) was localized at Jericho and had to come at the end of the same journey, although a journey from Galilee to Jerusalem cannot pass both through Samaria and Jericho. Here Luke has broken up a tract of parables (xviii. 1–14 and xix. 11–27) in order to insert a block of Marcan matter relating to the journey, apparently because the parable of the Pounds came to him with the localization of xix. 11. But the Good Samaritan and Martha and Mary seem to be inserted between two separate tracts, the mission of the Seventy and the sayings on prayer (x. 24 and xi. 1–13), for no particular reason. There may be a reason for the position of the widow's son at Nain (vii. 11 ff.; cf. above, p. 8, n. 2). But there seems none for the insertion of the anointing (vii. 36 ff.) between the Baptist's message (vii. 18 ff.) and the Marcan material (viii. 4–ix. 50). Similarly a block of unattached sayings and the ten lepers (xvii. 1–20) are inserted between the tract of parables which forms c. xvi and the apocalypse of xvii. 20–37. The fact that one of the lepers was a Samaritan may have suggested the location of that incident on the journey; there seems no reason for the insertion of xvii. 1–10, and it has no unity of subject or language to suggest that the sayings were combined before they reached Luke.

But a very large amount of the matter not found in Mark falls in Luke into groups of sayings, which generally are united by subject or verbal association, or in some cases by the fact that all are in the form of parables. There is normally a narrative introduction which may be simply formal but may introduce the main theme of the group of sayings which follow. The introduction is followed by the opening saying, to which further sayings are appended, introduced by the words 'and he said' or some equally colourless formula. There is frequently a question addressed to Jesus by the disciples or the bystanders to elicit some of the later sayings; the section usually concludes with a saying sounding a particularly dramatic or impressive note or serving to summarize the whole. This structure has already met us in such passages as Mark vii. 1–23 and ix.

It might be argued that at least one of these tracts formed part of the long Q compilation, namely the charge preserved by Luke as the charge to the Seventy (x. 1 ff.) and conflated by Matthew with the Marcan charge to the Twelve.[1] For in Luke the charge to the Seventy is immediately preceded by the answers of Jesus to the three candidates for discipleship (ix. 57 ff.).[2] In Matthew these appear (from the same written source) at viii. 19–22, where they are only separated from the healing of the centurion's servant by the healing of Peter's wife's mother. At this point Matthew is treating Mark with some freedom; he has transferred the healing of the leper (Matt. viii. 1–4 = Mark i. 40–5) to the end of the Sermon on the Mount. The new Torah is followed by a triad of cures: the leper,

---

[1] For this document see below, p. 48.

[2] The settings of the two incidents in Matthew (viii. 19–22) and Luke vary widely. On the other hand the words of the candidates are practically identical, while the first of the two answers is verbally identical in both. This identity is the more remarkable in view of the fact that the answer contains the quite impossible word κατασκηνώσεις for 'nests'. The verb κατασκηνοῦν is reasonable enough for birds settling in branches, as in Mark iv. 32, and has good LXX parallels (Ps. civ. 12 and Dan. (Th.) iv. 21); but the noun is impossibly stilted as meaning the nest or the temporary lodging place of a bird; in the LXX it is only used of the 'dwelling' of God in his temple. The explanation of its use here appears to be that the saying was translated from Aramaic into Greek by a Christian who knew the parable of the Grain of Mustard Seed in Mark iv. 32 and knew no better than to use the noun derived from the verb for this saying. The omission of Luke's third saying by Matthew may be due, as Creed suggests, to the fact that Luke had the saying of ix. 62 in isolation and brought it in here with 61 as an introduction. But the explanation might simply be that Matthew's copy was defective.

the centurion's servant, and Peter's wife's mother. Thereafter the departure from Capernaum (Matt. viii. 18 f.) may be due to the fact that the setting out on a journey seemed an appropriate place to introduce the scribe and the disciple who offer to follow Jesus. These answers are followed by a block of Marcan material up to Matt. ix. 26; then come the healing of two blind men and the curious fragment ix. 32–4; then comes the mission of the Twelve which is a conflation of the Marcan mission of the Twelve with the Lucan mission of the Seventy.

The Lucan Sermon is similarly followed by the healing of the centurion's servant; after this, except for the Baptist's message, which either Matthew or Luke has displaced (cf. above, p. 8), we have only matter proper to Luke and the Marcan section viii. 4– ix. 50 between the healing of the centurion's servant and the story of the candidates for discipleship.

On the other hand, it is more likely that the Lucan material between the Q section proper ending with the healing of the cen- turion's servant (Luke vii. 1–10) and the Marcan section beginning at viii. 4 represents a collection of material from different sources, the stories of the widow's son at Nain, the woman in Simon's house and the Samaritan village having all had an independent circulation. If so, it may have been Luke who combined the story of the candi- dates for discipleship (Luke ix. 57–62) with the non-Marcan charge to the disciples (x. 1 ff.); the severity of the conditions would then furnish an introduction to the austerity imposed on the missioners. In any event the Lucan charge to the Seventy, possibly preceded by the two or three sayings, seems to have been originally an indepen- dent unit, even if it had been compiled as part of Q before it reached the evangelists.

CHAPTER V

THE CHARGE TO THE DISCIPLES

Both Luke and Matthew had before them two versions of Jesus' charge to his disciples, apparently addressed to them on the occasion of some local proclamation of the kingdom to the Jewish population of Galilee (cf. Vol. I, p. 23).[1] The first (Mark vi. 7 ff.) came from Mark's Twelve-source, the second from the Q material. Matt. ix. 37 ff. conflates the two, and expands them with other material; Luke as usual avoids conflation, but has not felt free to omit the second charge, since it contained matter which he regarded as too valuable to be lost. Accordingly, Luke preserves the Marcan charge in its original place at ix. 1 ff. and inserts the Q version at x. 1 ff.

Both Luke and Matthew introduce into their versions of the Marcan charge some extension of the asceticism required of the disciples in the original. Early Christian missionaries soon invited comparison with the travelling Cynic preachers of the Hellenistic world, and it would seem that the necessity of competing with them led to the prohibition of the sandals which Mark emphatically allows.[2] At Mark vi. 9 the clumsy introduction of ἀλλὰ ὑποδεδεμένους σανδάλια between the ἵνα clause and the direct speech of μὴ ἐνδύσησθε suggests that Mark is aware of a growing tendency towards asceticism and has inserted the clause to combat it. Matthew (x. 10) inserts the prohibition of sandals from the Q source (=Luke

---

[1] Wellhausen and Bultmann (whose views are conveniently reported by Rawlinson on Mark vi. 7 ff. and Creed on Luke ix. 1 ff.) deny the historicity of the mission; this is *a priori* dogmatism of the least defensible kind. Whether they would regard as equally fictitious the messengers sent out by Alexander of Abonouteichos to proclaim the new oracle (Lucian, *Alexander* 24) does not appear.

[2] Cf. Musonius Rufus ap. Stob. *Anth.* III, 1, 209 (I. 84 Meineke; III, p. 174, ed. Wachsmuth and Hense): τοῦ γε ὑποδεδέσθαι τὸ ἀνυποδετεῖν τῷ δυναμένῳ κρεῖττον. According to Musonius it is better to have one χιτών rather than two, better still to have the ἱμάτιον alone. This was enough for Diogenes (Dio Chrys. VI, 14–15). The main roads of the Hellenistic world would be easier going than the rough tracks of Galilee; Clement of Alexandria thinks shoes justifiable on rough and hilly paths (*Paed.* II, 116, 2). Cf. also Athenaeus, *Deipn.* IV, 56, 163 E (a 'Pythagorean' cynic) and VI, 34, 238 A. For the comparison of Cynic and Christian preachers cf. Aelius Aristides, *Orat.* 46 (Dindorf, II, 394 f.); Origen, *c. Cels.* III, 50.

x. 4), and at ix. 3 Luke omits Mark's specific stress that sandals are to be worn, in this respect reconciling the instructions given in his two charges. On the other hand, the staff disallowed in the Marcan charge (Mark vi. 8, Luke ix. 3) does not receive special mention in Luke x. 4. It may be noticed that the Q version was consistent in its prohibition of shoes or sandals, since in Luke x. 11 the disciples are to wipe the dust off their bare feet; in Mark vi. 11 and parallels they are to 'shake' it off. Now it is probable that the gesture really consisted of shaking dust off the shoes, not off the feet (it is hard to imagine a dramatic gesture for the latter); if so the secondary character of the prohibition of sandals or shoes is clear.[1] Luke represents the Q charge as a charge to seventy disciples, who presumably symbolize the seventy nations of the world.[2] The number may be ascribed to Luke, as may the setting, which is quite inappropriate, since Jesus is going up to Jerusalem for his last journey. The 'coming' that the disciples were to proclaim was in any case not the coming of Jesus, but the coming of the kingdom of God.[3] Luke, indeed, by his insertion of ἑτέρους suggests that he is aware that he might be thought to be duplicating a story and is anxious to assure his readers that he is not.[4]

It is almost regarded as axiomatic that Matt. x. 5 f. and 23 are due either to anti-Gentile editing by Matthew or to his use of sources which were not interested in Gentile converts (see Allen, *ad loc.*) or

[1] Cf. Cadbury in Jackson and Lake, *Beginnings of Christianity*, v, 270, where Dalman is quoted as saying that the custom of shaking dust off shoes or garments survives in Palestine to the present day.

[2] Cf. Creed *ad loc.* For the variant seventy-two cf. *Jerusalem*, p. 177, n. 23; for this regular confusion between seventy (the number of the Mosaic elders, who make seventy-two with Moses and Aaron included) and seventy-two (six from each tribe), cf. Clem. Alex. *Strom.* I, 21, 142 (404) and Jacoby's note (*F.G.H.* 70 F 236) quoting seventy-two constellations (Pliny), countries (Horapollon) and satrapies of the Seleucid Empire (Appian). In *Jerusalem* I suggest that Luke derived his seventy (or seventy-two) from the original presbyters of the Church of Jerusalem; but it is temerarious to seek any source beyond the nations of the world. For Rabbinic traditions cf. Str.-B. III, pp. 48 ff.

[3] It is possible that Luke's source represented this as the purpose of the mission: in Mark iii. 14, which is really the introduction to vi. 9 ff. in the Twelve source, they were sent κηρύσσειν (τὸ εὐαγγέλιον, actually read by DW and the old Latin, or τὴν βασιλείαν being understood).

[4] Luke is probably responsible for the rather pretentious ἀνέδειξεν in x. 1; cf. Polybius XXI, 21, 3 (Hultsch) and Dittenberger, *O.G.I.S.* 73, 7; also the vocabulary in Welles, *Royal Correspondence in the Hellenistic Period*.

definitely opposed to the Gentile mission.[1] It is undeniable that Matthew might have drawn his version of the charge from his anti-Gentile source, though in that case we ought to have ἐθνικῶν instead of ἐθνῶν (see above, p. 33, n. 1); but the change might be due to careless copying. On the other hand, this does not explain 16 b, which is a hard saying when it is contrasted with 9 f. and 19 and the general attitude of the early Christian missionaries; Kilpatrick (p. 98) regards it as a 'hortatory addition to a Q saying' but overlooks its difficulty.[2] It is easier to suppose that Luke omitted a saying of this kind because he failed to understand it, than that Matthew inserted it.

If we look at the Matthean version of the charge as a duplicate of the Marcan version, preserved in a rather fuller form, it is noticeable that it fits in admirably with the situation. Jesus sends out the Twelve with specific directions: 'I do not want you to go outside Galilee into the Gentile regions on its borders or the Gentile cities in it, nor yet into Samaria; proclaim that the kingdom of God is at hand. Take nothing with you and stay with any one who will entertain you. You are going on a dangerous mission; be as wise as serpents in avoiding anything that might be used as an accusation against you, and as innocent as doves in avoiding any just cause of offence. You are quite likely to be arrested and beaten in the synagogues; if so, do not be anxious; you will be inspired to give a good defence to all accusations.' (There may be a genuine core in Matt. x. 17–22; for the most part it is a secondary compilation, composed of sayings belonging to other occasions.) 'If you are persecuted in one city flee to the next; you will not be able to go through the whole of Galilee before the appointed time.' Here the appointed time would originally have referred to some date by which the Twelve were to finish their journey and return to Jesus at an agreed rendezvous; it would almost automatically be changed into the Parousia in the first Christian generation.

The omission of the local restrictions by Luke in a charge which he intends by his introduction of the Seventy to be a symbol of the

---

[1] Kilpatrick (*Origins*, p. 119) argues that in Matt. x. 23 the cities of Israel are all cities with Jewish colonies; but this does not explain 5f.

[2] Str.-B. give a relatively late Jewish parallel (R. Judah b. Simon, c. A.D. 320): Wetstein adds nothing. Allen *ad loc.* quotes no parallel saying. The difficulty is that normally a snake stands for evil; cf. Matt. xxiii. 33, II Cor. xi. 3, Rev. xii. 9, Philo, *Leg. Alleg.* II, 74 ff.

mission to the Gentiles would be natural and inevitable; their preservation in circles which had little or no enthusiasm for that mission
would be equally likely. It is, of course, arguable that the limitation
was introduced by violently anti-Gentile circles, but it is doubtful
whether they would have been content with such moderate language;
it is more probable that we have in Matt. x. 5 f., 16 b and 23 a genuine
record of the actual directions of Jesus, though the charge as a whole
has been largely amplified by Matthew with material drawn from
other sources, while the last clause of 23 has been rewritten in the
apocalyptic vein which has been introduced at 17 ff.

The Lucan charge may therefore be secondary in so far as it omits
the local limitations, though Luke cannot be blamed for omitting
them in view of the fact that they only referred to a specific occasion.
The versions of the charge in Matthew and Luke both contain features
which may be regarded as primitive, while they have both undergone
modifications. The saying about the harvest (Luke x. 2=Matt.
ix. 37 f.) is preserved by Luke in the position which it held in the
source; Matthew has transferred it to an earlier position in order to
make it clear that the appointment of the Twelve is necessitated by
the need of evangelization; originally no doubt the saying was a
detached fragment of tradition, which the source put at the beginning
of the charge. Luke x. 3 probably also stood in the position he has
given it; but he has cut out the unedifying command to be as prudent
as serpents; after all, it was the Pauline tradition that the disciple
must be a fool for Christ's sake (I Cor. iv. 10). Matthew, however,
has displaced the whole verse and made it into an introduction to the
warning of the dangers that await the disciples; this warning was
originally merely a warning of the dangers that awaited them in the
synagogues of Galilee. Luke has omitted the original warning with
the rest of the local colouring; Matthew has rewritten it from Mark
xiii. 9, for which he has a much weaker version at xxiv. 8. But it is
doubtful whether he would have made the transfer if there had been
nothing to justify it in his source. Matthew substitutes 'city or
village' for the 'house' of Mark vi. 10 which also appeared in the Q
version (Luke x. 5); that version also had injunctions for behaviour
on entering a city (Luke x. 8), but Matthew substitutes the city or
village for the house and adds the command to inquire who in it is
worthy, a command which is meaningless in the supposed setting

and must be drawn from the later days of the Church, when it could be generally assumed that you would find Christians or at least Jewish sympathizers wherever you went. The conception of 'your peace' as a word of power which can rest upon a house or return, according to the worthiness of the inmates, has a very primitive and Semitic air,[1] as has Luke's 'son of peace'. In x. 7 Luke has probably preserved the correct position for the saying 'The labourer is worthy of his hire', while in 8 ff. he has preserved a good Semitic parallelism between the city that receives the disciples and the city that rejects them.[2] On the other hand in its present form this section (Luke x. 8 f.) has suffered from a clumsy modification in the command 'eat what is set before you' as applied to the entering into a city, as if the disciples were likely to be offered public entertainment, or be tempted to complain of it if it were unsatisfactory. The insertion is hardly likely to have been made by Luke; it has clearly been inserted by someone who wanted to introduce a parallelism between entering a house in *v*. 7 and entering a city in *v*. 8. It would seem that originally the charge covered two points, conduct towards houses where the disciples are entertained and conduct towards places which accept or reject them. The bare outlines of this charge have survived in Mark; in Matthew and Luke we have a fuller version, which may be older than the Marcan form. Conduct on entering a house is covered by Luke x. 5–7, while 8–11 in Luke are an expanded version of the charge with regard to particular places. That the places are 'cities' is a reflexion of the later conditions of Christian missions, as is the phrase 'going out into the streets'. As against this Luke has preserved the original ending of *v*. 11 which corresponds with that of *v*. 9. The original form of this part of the charge will have been roughly: καὶ εἰς ὃν ἂν τόπον εἰσέρχησθε καὶ δέχωνται ὑμᾶς, θεραπεύετε τοὺς ἐν αὐτῷ ἀσθενεῖς, καὶ λέγετε αὐτοῖς· ἤγγικεν ἡ βασιλεία τοῦ θεοῦ. καὶ εἰς ὃν ἂν τόπον εἰσέρχησθε καὶ μὴ δέχωνται ὑμᾶς, ἐκπορεύεσθε ἐκεῖθεν καὶ λέγετε αὐτοῖς· καὶ τὸν κονιορτὸν ἐκ τῶν

---

[1] For this power of a word cf. Isa. lv. 11; Moore, *Judaism*, 1, 414.

[2] The Marcan version of the charge at vi. 10 only envisages single houses, but at vi. 11 we have an extremely clumsy allusion to 'a place which does not receive you and they do not hear you'. It looks as though behind the Marcan version there was a fuller one which recognized the corporate guilt of the place as well as that of the single house and it is quite likely that the Q version in this respect stood nearer to the original. Matthew's attempt to combine the two in xiv. 14 is even clumsier.

ποδῶν ἐκτινάσσομεν ὑμῖν. πλὴν τοῦτο γινώσκετε ὅτι ἤγγικεν ἡ βασιλεία τοῦ θεοῦ.

It is of interest to note that Matthew by his compression has lost the good Semitic parallelism which Luke has on the whole preserved, though he has somewhat overloaded the wording; on the other hand Matthew's compression has not only spoilt the parallelism but has left the allusion to 'departing from that house or city' quite meaningless. It would appear that we have in Matthew and Luke not a mere expansion of Mark but a quite independent version, which retained a better version of the original charge.

The woes on the cities of Galilee formed part of the source which contained the charge; Luke (x. 12 ff.) inserts them in full at this point, while Matthew (x. 15) gives only the opening saying with its warning from the fate of Sodom. He has transferred the rest to xi. 20 ff. after the Baptist's message. His reason for doing so was that he had decided to expand the original charge from its local and temporary form into a general charge given by the exalted Christ to all Christian missionaries working under the shadow of the persecution, which was to be followed by the Second Coming. For this purpose he transfers verse 16 from its proper position and makes it serve as an introduction to his warnings as to the coming persecutions. The following verse, x. 23, comes from the original, though the allusion to 'cities of Israel' has become unintelligible. Of the rest it would seem that Matt. x. 40 formed the original end of the charge, though probably in its Lucan wording (Luke x. 16), since Matthew assimilates the wording to Mark ix. 37, and then on his own account appends two floating sayings (x. 41–2) lacking any proper place in the charge but connected in form and content with its closing sentence. Verse 41 is purely Matthean, and the interest and emphasis of both 40 and 41 is significantly different. Luke's originality is shown by the fact that his ending for the charge is an encouragement to the apostolic missionaries; whereas Matthew is more interested in encouraging those who may offer them hospitality, an anxiety which reflects a later situation.

Matthew gives elsewhere (xi. 21–3) an enlarged version of the whole of the warnings to the rather obscure cities of Galilee, preserved by Luke at the conclusion of the charge to the Seventy (Luke x. 13 ff.). Matthew must have thought them inappropriate in this position, the more so since, according to the editorial verse Matt. xi. 1, Jesus was just going to preach in them. Accordingly he found these warnings left on his hands and, in order to dispose of them as quickly as possible, transferred them to the end of his next block of material, the answer to the Baptist's question (Matt. xi. 2–19), where they form a good continuation of the denunciation of 'this generation'. This hypothesis is fortified by the repetition of the allusion to Sodom in Matt. xi. 24, which betrays that this section has been moved from its place in the source.[1]

Luke preserves the original charge virtually as it reached him, except that he has eliminated the purely local limitations and the allusion to the wisdom of serpents. Though the position for the charge is not very appropriate, he may well have inserted the whole section here precisely because the concluding woes already attached to it seemed to fit the final departure of Jesus from Galilee. The question remains open whether the source was right in attaching the woes on the cities to the Mission (of the Twelve). All that can be said is that it is by no means inconceivable. The mission may have been sent out by Jesus to the villages and towns of Galilee which he had not visited, at a stage in the ministry when it had become clear that there was no further hope of a general movement in favour of the gospel in the narrow field of Capernaum, Bethsaida, and Chorazin.[2] If this is so, then the charge in its non-Marcan version has preserved a genuine historical reminiscence, which Mark has lost. Naturally the Matthean expansions, inserted between x. 23 and the end, apart from 40, have no claim to be part of the document which he shares with Luke. Matt. x. 26 ff. is preserved in its original literary context at Luke xii. 2 ff., where it forms part of an independent collection of sayings (cf. below, p. 66). Matt. x. 34 ff. appears in Luke (xii. 51 ff.), apparently as a detached saying. From x. 37 to the end we have sayings which reappear in Mark in various contexts, while 38 was also current in the non-Marcan tradition, in which it was associated with 'hating father and mother' (Luke xiv. 26 ff.).

[1] Note the tell-tale ἀνεκτότερον at Matt. x. 15 and xi. 24, and Luke x. 12; the word is not Septuagintal, and does not appear elsewhere in the New Testament (except Matt. xi. 22).

[2] For the probable sites of these towns see articles in Hastings' *Dictionary of the Bible*. They are close to one another at the north end of the sea of Galilee; a wider appeal to Galilee would have been inevitable at some period.

Here again its Lucan position as one of a collection of unattached sayings is original as against its Matthean position.

It is worth asking further whether the 'Johannine saying' of Luke x. 21 ff. (= Matt. xi. 25 ff.) may not have been attached to the mission of the Twelve before it reached Luke and Matthew. In Luke the connexion is broken by the insertion of 18–20, which would appear to have been an independent block of matter; if it stood in the source common to Matthew and Luke it is hard to explain its omission by Matthew. It is of course possible that it had been inserted in Luke's version of the source before it reached him; in any event the non-Lucan πλήν suggests that we are dealing with material which is not of Luke's invention, though no doubt the setting given in x. 17 is editorial.[1] But two facts point to the conclusion that the great thanksgiving was originally attached to the mission: Matthew places it immediately after the woes on the cities, and although, as we have seen, he has transferred these from their original position, it is at least possible that he associated the woes with the thanksgiving because they stood together in his source. Luke for his part attaches the thanksgiving to the return of the disciples (where he has rewritten x. 17 and inserted 18 ff.); Matthew entirely forgets to mention this, his 'charge' having by the end lost all connexion with history; the acceptance of the Gospel by the simple villagers of the countryside, as against its rejection by the more sophisticated people of the towns, would furnish a good introduction to the contrast between the 'wise and prudent' and the 'babes' of Luke x. 21.

Naturally it need not be supposed that this connexion must go back to the ministry of Jesus; probably the thanksgiving had an independent existence as an unattached saying before it was associated with the sending and return of the disciples. But the thanksgiving forms an admirable conclusion to the charge and the return to tell Jesus of the success of their mission.[2] There will have been a

---

[1] Both ὑποτάσσω and ὑποστρέφω are peculiar to Luke, Paul, and the Hellenistic New Testament writers, except for Mark xiv. 40 where, however, ὑπόστρεψας is omitted by אB. The verses that follow are highly Semitic in content; besides the Old Testament parallels cf. Str.-B. *ad loc.*; also *Test. Lev.* xviii. 12; I Enoch xlvii. 3.

[2] For the logion itself cf. *Hellenistic Elements*, p. 6. Norden's view (*Agnostos Theos*, pp. 277 ff.) that the logion follows a fixed scheme of preaching suffers from the disadvantage that he has to make the closing invitation of Matt. xi. 28 ff. part of the original saying. There is no conceivable reason why Luke should have

mention of the return of the disciples, which Luke has rewritten in order to introduce the fall of Satan from heaven, possibly because x. 21 gives thanks for a 'revelation' while without this passage there is no obvious revelation in the story. The 'makarism' of Luke x. 23 would provide an excellent conclusion to the whole episode of the sending and return of the disciples. No doubt it was originally an independent saying, but the original compiler regarded it as a suitable conclusion to the whole. Luke has simply copied out his source without noticing that properly speaking 'the disciples' to whom Jesus turns and speaks privately ought to be the Twelve to the exclusion of the Seventy who have just returned; the improbability of such a proceeding needs no demonstration, but such failures to harmonize his sources are entirely in the Lucan manner.[1]

The verbal agreement, amounting to almost exact identity, between Matt. ix. 37 b and 35 and Luke x. 2; Matt. xi. 21–3 and Luke x. 13–14; and again Matt. xi. 25 b–27 and Luke x. 21 b–22, makes it clear that the two versions are drawn from a common

omitted it and failed to reproduce it elsewhere; on the other hand Matthew is fond of rearranging his material (cf. Kilpatrick, *Origins*, p. 27). The verbal agreement between Matthew and Luke in the preceding verses rules out the possibility of different sources. It should further be noted that Norden's 'scheme' of revelation, thanksgiving and appeal to men, which he finds both in this logion and *Corp. Herm.* I, involves a rearrangement of the Hermetic tract, in which in the MSS. the appeal comes before the thanksgiving. (The difficulty was pointed out to me by Professor C. H. Dodd.) Naturally the extent to which the words can be regarded as an authentic saying cannot be decided on critical grounds; whether the Messianic consciousness of Jesus would have led him to speak as in Luke x. 22 depends on our subjective view of the probabilities. Cf. below, pp. 138 ff.

[1] At one point interference with the source may be suspected. At x. 24 Creed (*ad loc.*) regards Luke's 'kings' as more forcible (and therefore more original?) than Matthew's 'righteous men' (xiii. 17). But there is no clear reason why Matthew should have changed it. On the other hand kings are the proper recipients of Hellenistic revelations, their souls being nearer to the divine than those of ordinary mortals. Cf. *P.M.G.* XIII, 227: τούτων τὴν ἀκάματον λύσιν καὶ θεοφιλῆ προσεφώνησά σοι, τέκνον, ἣν οὐδὲ βασιλεῖς ἴσχυσαν καταλαβέσθαι. Also Manilius I, 41 with Housman's note, and *Corp. Herm.*: *Exc. Stob.* xxiv; the notion is discussed by F. Boll, *Aus der Offenbarung Johannis* (1914), pp. 136–42; F. Cumont, *L'Égypte des Astrologues* (1937), pp. 26–7; A. J. Festugière, *La Révélation d'Hermès Trismégiste*, I, pp. 324 ff. Moreover, not many of the kings of Israel and Judah would have 'desired to see these things'; David, Solomon in his better period, Hezekiah and Josiah are about the only possible candidates. But there were many righteous men looking for the Consolation of Israel. It seems that here Luke has changed his source to conform to the Hellenistic convention.

written source. As a collection it corresponds well in its Lucan form to the 'tract' type. We have a slight narrative introduction, followed by a connected discourse; in this case there is no more reason than in most to suppose that it reproduces an original unit of discourse, based on a genuine historical situation. The question which interrupts or follows the discourse is replaced by the return of the disciples; possibly Luke inserted their words in order to conform to the general pattern of his sources and used the occasion as an opening for bringing in 18 ff. The interruption leads to a fresh set of sayings with a highly suitable dramatic conclusion. Thus, even if it came to Luke and Matthew as part of a continuous Q, it would seem to have had an earlier history as a separate tract.

The end of this section is followed by the parable of the good Samaritan (x. 25 ff.) and the story of Mary and Martha (x. 38 ff.). The opening of the parable of the good Samaritan offers a peculiar problem. The Lucan story has obvious affinities with that of Mark xii. 28 ff., which Luke omits, presumably because he regards it as a doublet of his own version.[1] On the other hand he agrees with Matthew against Mark in saying that the questioner was 'tempting' Jesus. The evangelists differ in their description of the questioner. Mark has 'one of the scribes'. Luke calls him νομικός, which also appears in almost all texts of Matthew; but there its omission by fam. 1 e syr. sin. Arm. Georg. Orig. seems certainly correct, so that this cannot also be reckoned to be an agreement of Matthew and Luke against Mark.[2] Further, there seems to be some connexion between the introduction to the parable of the good Samaritan and the story of the rich man of Mark x. 17 ff. (a young man according to Matt. xix. 22, a ruler according to Luke xviii. 18), since both in Luke x. 25 and in Mark x. 17 the question asked is 'What shall I do to inherit eternal life?' The problem is complicated by the fact that the Lucan introduction to the parable of the good Samaritan is a complete story in itself, 'this do and thou shalt live' being a perfectly good answer to the original question. Evidently the story of Mark xii. 28 ff. circulated in a variant version, which may well have been nearer to

[1] The wording of Mark xii. 28–31 and Luke x. 25–8 is very different; apart from the Shema the only word common to both is αὐτόν. Yet the form of the question in Mark x. 17 and Luke x. 25 is virtually identical apart from the omission of ἀγαθέ.

[2] Cf. Streeter, *The Four Gospels*, p. 320; Kilpatrick in *J.T.S.* n.s., 1 (1950), p. 57.

the original, in which the questioner was a lawyer and the question asked related to inheriting eternal life. But it is entirely possible that the form of the question had been affected by the story of Mark x. 17 ff. at an earlier stage of the tradition, if indeed we have not here divergent versions of what was historically the same incident. Both stories presuppose that the person who converses with Jesus concerning the Ten Commandments stands in a friendly relation to him, which is a pointer that an authentic historical reminiscence is being preserved. Matthew (xxii. 34–40) has retained the story of Mark xii. 28–31 in its Marcan position and naturally omitted the Lucan version; he may have introduced 'tempting him' from the doublet, or he may simply have assumed that anyone who asked Jesus a question was tempting him. By contrast Luke preserves the non-Marcan story intact, but omits the doublet.

A further problem is raised by the association of the question about eternal life with the parable of the good Samaritan. The parable does not really suit the introduction since it deals with the difference between real and conventional standards of goodness, not with the universality of the law of loving your neighbour (cf. Smith, p. 53). It would be tempting to suppose that the good Samaritan is drawn from a tract containing a collection of incidents dealing with Jesus' relations with Samaritans, and it would favour such a view that the parable comes in close proximity to the incident of Luke ix. 51 ff., the break between them being due to the necessity of bringing the mission of the Seventy as near as possible to Jesus' departure from Galilee. On the other hand it seems a serious objection that the incident of the Samaritan leper in Luke xvii. 11 ff. would naturally come from such a collection if it existed, and there seems no reason for its separation from the rest of the Samaritan material. Nor does this hypothesis explain the clumsy connexion between the question as to the commandments and the parable. It is more probable that the section Luke x. 25–37 was part of a compilation in which the answer of x. 28 was followed by the words 'And Jesus said'; 29 is simply due to Luke's desire to provide a connected narrative. It is of course unlikely that the compilation consisted simply of these two incidents; but it may have contained other matter which Luke has omitted, presumably because it occurred in his other sources as well. The story itself shows signs of considerable Lucan editing, but

Creed's view that 'the idiomatic vocabulary and artistic finish of the verses 30–5 point to the story having been actually composed in the language in which we now read it' overstates the case; as a matter of fact the string of participles looks like a superficial attempt to get rid of the parataxis of a Semitic original.[1] Other idioms may be due to Lucan editing, but they are such as could easily be inserted by a reviser (οἳ καί in 30, προσδαπανᾶν and ἐπανέρχεσθαι in 35).

The story which follows (Luke x. 38 ff.) appears to have come to Luke as an independent fragment, which he inserted here partly to increase the effect of his narrative as a travel-story, partly because it served to introduce the teaching on prayer. It would seem that originally the answer of Jesus read ὀλίγων δέ ἐστιν χρεία, and was a simple rebuke to Martha for her anxiety and fussiness. But at a very early date this was regarded as unsatisfactory and ἢ ἑνός was inserted to give the saying a spiritual meaning applicable not merely to the particular occasion but to all time; the extreme clumsiness of the resulting text led to the omission of the whole clause by D, the old Latin and syr. sin., and the substitution of ἑνὸς δέ by the majority of manuscripts, including 𝔓⁴⁵. The manuscript support for ὀλίγων δέ ἐστιν χρεία is very slight, but the view that it was original explains the various readings; it can only be advanced as perhaps the most probable explanation of the confusion. There seems no reason why ἑνὸς δέ should ever have been changed and the ὀλίγων δέ ἐστιν χρεία ἢ ἑνός of ℵB, etc., seems meaningless (cf. Creed *ad loc.*). If this explanation is correct Luke has preserved a story whose authenticity is guaranteed by its need of improvement before it could give a suitably edifying lesson.

[1] Note the quite otiose ἀπῆλθον ἀφέντες of 30 and the triple repetition of the unnecessary ἰδών in 31–3; the four repetitions of αὐτός in 34 are thoroughly bad. Luke seems to have revised his source here by substituting participles for main verbs; but he is hopelessly inconsistent in such matters. Thus in viii. 25 we have φοβηθέντες ἐθαύμασαν λέγοντες for ἐφοβήθησαν καὶ ἔλεγον and in viii. 41 b πεσὼν παρεκάλει for πίπτει καὶ παρεκάλει in Mark; cf. xx. 27 as against Mark xii. 18. But he has left the widow's son at Nain untouched. On the other hand in vi. 6 b we have a shocking parataxis as against Mark iii. 1 b, and in viii. 41 a the introduction of Jairus is definitely worse than Mark's. It would seem that in the last two passages Luke has Mark's source before him as well as Mark and out of sheer carelessness incorporates the inferior version. And in x. 31 κατέβαινεν ἐν τῇ ὁδῷ seems quite indefensible (contrast x. 4, Acts viii. 36 and xxv. 3). It is tolerable of a conversation which takes place during a journey as in Luke ix. 57, xxiv. 32 and 35, but not of going along a road.

CHAPTER VI

A TRACT ON PRAYER

The section which follows the story of Martha and Mary (Luke xi. 1–13) appears to be a separate document dealing with prayer; it is shorter than most, and has no interruption or question in the later part to elicit an interpretation or expansion of what has gone before; naturally it is possible that Luke has omitted part of his material; there is no reason to suppose that various tracts did not overlap one another in more cases than we can detect. Otherwise it follows the type, with a narrative introduction to introduce the opening saying or group of sayings, a further group introduced with 'and he said' at xi. 5 and a new group at xi. 9 where the 'and I say unto you' may represent an original 'and he said'. Matthew's treatment of the source is typical; he has taken the Lord's Prayer (Matt. vi. 9–13) and appended it, not very aptly, to the teaching on prayer contained in his triadic source, as expanded from the anti-Gentile source. The parable of the importunate friend could hardly be harmonized with the general style of the Sermon on the Mount which has nothing in the nature of a formal parable (as against parabolic comparisons which are little more than metaphors)[1] until the conclusion, the parable of the two houses. It would seem that Matthew wished to finish off this particular source; so he includes the closing section (Luke xi. 9 ff. = Matt. vii. 7 ff.) at the end of the Sermon on the Mount after the parable of the mote and the beam from the Lucan Sermon and before the eschatological conclusion, and omits the importunate friend completely.[2]

It need hardly be pointed out that a written or fixed oral homily on prayer, containing the words of the Lord's Prayer and an exhortation to perseverance with a promise of the reward of such perseverance, would be a natural and necessary part of the equipment of the primitive missionary or catechist. The variations in the text of the Lord's

---

[1] For the varieties in parabolic types cf. Dodd, *Parables of the Kingdom*, pp. 16 f. and Smith, *Parables of the Synoptic Gospels*, ch. 1.

[2] For the correct text of the Lord's Prayer and the last clause of xi. 13 cf. above, p. 26, n. 1.

Prayer are remarkable, but easily understood. The prayer no doubt existed in the liturgical use of the Church quite apart from the tract, and Matthew has substituted the version of his own Church for that of the source, the longer Matthean version being presumably an expansion of the original.

It is of course likely enough that the narrative introduction xi. 1 owes something to Lucan editing. Thus Luke emphasizes Jesus' prayer, as Creed rightly notes (*op. cit.* pp. 155–6). Although it is exaggerated to call the Semitic καὶ ἐγένετο a 'characteristic' Lucan construction, since Luke never uses it in Acts, and it is frequent in Mark, appearing five times also in Matthew, yet it seems that Luke uses it as having a hieratic ring,[1] and he may have introduced it here, though it is possible that in the cases where he introduces it into his revision of Mark without any excuse, he is following Mark's source rather than Mark himself. Nevertheless, it is quite likely that he himself has rewritten the introduction; incidentally it may be observed that xi. 1 might be the question which usually comes near the end of a collection, and that the whole of the original opening has been omitted.

[1] Cf. my *Acts of the Apostles*, pp. 6 ff.; Bultmann, *Geschichte*, p. 385.

CHAPTER VII

THE CONTROVERSY CONCERNING MIRACLES

The section of Luke (xi. 14–32) following the tract on prayer is a composite document with a considerable history behind it. It appears to have reached Luke in its present form; there seems to be no reason why he should have inserted verse 16, which as it stands is a rather inept anticipation of 29–32. The difficulty, however, vanishes when it is recognized that the whole passage is a compilation for the use of Christian controversialists, who have to face the Jewish objections (*a*) that Jesus cast out devils by Beelzebub, and (*b*) that he never wrought a really convincing miracle. This does not mean that the sayings in this section cannot be genuine; there is no reason to doubt that arguments of this kind were brought against Jesus in his lifetime. But they have been collected in their present form because they met two objections which must have been extremely frequent. It is probable that 14–28 once formed a separate unit in their present form; the interruption and answer in the last verse would form a suitable conclusion; if so there has been an intermediate stage of compilation before the tract reached the evangelist.

It is generally agreed that Luke is here following a non-Marcan source, although Mark records the incident.[1] There is the bare minimum of verbal similarity between the two Gospels throughout the sections common to both. The non-Marcan version seems to have contained primitive features (note the 'finger of God' in 20), while on the other hand it ascribes to Jesus a magical power to read men's thoughts[2] which is not found in Mark. It is of course perfectly reasonable to suppose that Jesus possessed a remarkable 'prophetic' power of insight into men's minds; the point is that the emphasis

---

[1] For the whole passage in its relation to Mark cf. Creed *ad loc.*

[2] Cf. *Gentiles*, p. 71, and add *P.M.G.* III, 265 to the references there given. In general Mark does not go beyond a prophetic insight into men's thoughts (ii. 8 by itself need mean no more). In the later evangelists it is much enhanced; but a comparison of Luke xi. 17 and Matt. xii. 25 shows that the enhancement goes back to their source at this point.

laid on it in such passages as this tends to assimilate his power to that of the conventional magician. Matthew has conflated the two accounts after his usual manner; it is interesting to observe that he has actually detached the opening story of an exorcism from the non-Marcan version and inserted it at Matt. ix. 32, apparently because he was inserting the saying on Beelzebub of x. 25, which in Mark iii. 20 ff. immediately precedes the Beelzebub controversy, into the charge to the Twelve and therefore some statement that Jesus, the master of the house, had been identified with Beelzebub was needed earlier.

An interesting point with regard to the controversy is that both the Marcan and the non-Marcan accounts lead up to a saying about Jesus' relations with his family. In the case of the Marcan account we should naturally suppose that Mark had the two stories before him as independent units, and that the amalgamation of the two is merely the consequence of Mark's editorial methods. But Luke has preserved the Marcan story as an independent unit separated from the Beelzebub controversy at viii. 19 ff.; it follows instead of preceding the parable of the Sower, but this is probably due to mere inadvertence in compilation; in any event Luke had no objection to it. But the Lucan version of the controversy leads up to a story in which the setting is entirely different, though the saying of Jesus is more or less a variation of the Marcan story. Thus it would seem that both versions had been associated with sayings about the true kindred of Jesus from a period earlier than the original form of the tradition from which both the Marcan and the non-Marcan versions are derived, although there is nothing in the Beelzebub controversy to make either the saying concerning the true kindred of Jesus or the Lucan story particularly appropriate in the context.[1]

The section which follows (Luke xi. 29–32) had already, it would seem, been attached to that which precedes it by the inclusion of the demand for a sign from heaven before it reached Luke and Matthew, who have done their best to obscure the point by the insertion of formal narrative introductions to the demand for a sign from heaven.

---

[1] The most satisfactory explanation seems to be that we have a genuine reminiscence of the actual order of the incidents related, in the sense that there was a tradition that the argument about Beelzebub was followed by a saying in which the true kinsfolk of Jesus were declared to be his disciples or in which those who heard and kept the word of God were declared to be blessed rather than his mother.

Matthew has completed his task by eliminating the demand for a sign from the opening incidents of the Beelzebub controversy entirely and introducing the demand for a sign as a completely new request from some of the scribes and Pharisees. Luke has been less successful: the opening of xi. 29 implies that we are beginning a completely new episode; in fact there was already a crowd present in 27, but Luke has ignored the fact and introduced a scrap of editorial narrative which breaks the unity of the source as a whole, although that unity is presupposed by the demand for a sign in 16.[1]

The sayings themselves are a curious composition. In the tradition known to Mark there was only a demand for a sign and a blunt refusal (Mark viii. 11 ff.). The non-Marcan tradition, however, knew the sayings about the Queen of the South and the men of Nineveh (Luke xi. 31–2) and apparently expanded the original refusal of a sign in the sense of Luke xi. 29 b and 30, meaning that there would be given no sign except the preaching of repentance by the Son of Man, just as Nineveh was given no sign but the preaching of Jonah. A quite different expansion is given in the text of Matt. xii. 40, where Jonah becomes a type of the resurrection; but this is a problem in itself.[2] The phenomena in Luke are to be explained by the hypothesis that the refusal of a sign was coupled at a very early period of the tradition with the sayings about the Queen of the South and the men of Nineveh; thus the 'sign of Jonah' is really derived from the saying about the men of Nineveh.

It has been suggested that the original words of Jesus referred not to the sign of Jonah but to the sign of John: no sign would be given

---

[1] Creed *ad loc.* follows Loisy in holding that Luke inserts verse 16 'to show that Christ's healings of the possessed have the force of a sign to those who can read them aright'. This seems most unlikely. The narrative statement of 29 is just the sort of narrative-link which Luke is fond of introducing in order to break the monotony of a string of sayings, though sometimes such narrative-links are quite unsuitable (cf. xii. 1, xiv. 25). It is hardly likely that he would (*a*) have introduced 16 in order to unite two separate pericopae, and then (*b*) have dissociated them by the narrative opening of 29. But to leave 16 standing as it was in his source and then to diversify his narrative by the opening words of 29, in spite of the fact that they break the connexion, is typical of Luke's slovenliness in revising his sources.

[2] Stendahl (*School of St Matthew*, pp. 132–3) pertinently observes that the argument of Justin (*Dial.* 107), that the allusion to the sign of Jonah was a *veiled* reference to the resurrection, presupposes his ignorance of Matt. xii. 40, which may therefore be an early interpolation. But he may have had Luke xi. 30 before him and simply forgotten the Matthean text; Justin's intelligence can be over-estimated.

to this generation other than the Baptist's preaching.[1] It is a difficulty for this view that Mark viii. 12 has lost the allusion to John the
Baptist; it seems hardly likely that the Baptist would have dis-
appeared from the Marcan tradition if he had been there originally.
But the objection might be met by supposing that the corruption of
'John' into 'Jonah' goes back to a pre-Marcan stage of the tradition,
and that Mark himself found the refusal of a sign coupled with a
reference to the sign of Jonah the prophet and omitted the allusion
because it did not seem to him relevant or intelligible. The Lucan
order in which the saying on the Queen of the South precedes that
on the sign of Jonah is presumably original, following as it does the
historical sequence; the order in Matthew with the two sayings about
Jonah connected and that on the Queen of the South following them
is more logical and therefore secondary.

The sentences which follow (Luke xi. 33–6) are peculiar. Luke
xi. 33 also came to the evangelist as part of Mark and was duly included at viii. 16 f. It would seem that he repeats them here because
they came to him with 34 ff. (cf. above, p. 18). But there is no reason
to suppose that they formed part of the tract which precedes them.
At any rate they are not likely to have formed an original part of it.
They would seem to have been unattached sayings, which might
have been inserted anywhere; but whether their present position
is due to the evangelist or to some previous reviser of the source
cannot be said.

The warnings against the scribes (Luke xi. 37–52) have been
discussed in Vol. I, pp. 94 ff.

[1] J. H. Michael in *J.T.S.* xxi (1920), pp. 146–59.

CHAPTER VIII

PREACHING THE GOSPEL AND WORLDLY RICHES

The section that follows the warnings against the scribes (Luke xi. 53–xii. 53) seems at first sight to have no single subject. On the other hand it has every claim to represent the original order of the source as against Matthew. The teaching, apart from the introductory narrative matter of xi. 53–xii. 1, which will be considered later (p. 68), consists of the exhortation to fearless preaching (Luke xii. 2–9) which Matthew has transferred bodily to the mission charge. This is followed by the saying of blasphemy against the Holy Ghost, which appears in Mark in the Beelzebub controversy; it would seem that the saying circulated in two settings. Matthew has conflated the Marcan and non-Marcan forms of the saying in his composite account of the Beelzebub controversy; it would seem that Luke found it in its present position in his source, where it is not particularly apposite. The connexion between denying Christ before men and blaspheming against him and the Holy Ghost has a certain association of ideas, but not such as would naturally lead Luke to transfer it from its Marcan position to the present one, and the verbal agreement is no more than is necessary if the saying was to be preserved with its original meaning. It would seem that like the saying of xii. 8 f. this saying circulated both in the Marcan and the non-Marcan tradition, since xii. 8 f. is a variant of the saying of Mark viii. 38 which Luke has preserved in his parallel (ix. 26) because at that point he is following Mark; no doubt the saying of xii. 10 would have appeared twice in Luke but for the fact that it occurs in Mark in the Beelzebub controversy, and here he is not following Mark at all. In 11 f. we have a doublet of the saying of Mark xiii. 11 (=Luke xxi. 14 f.).

At this point we break off into an entirely new set of sayings (Luke xii. 13 ff.), started by the request of one of the bystanders (who have presumably been waiting during Jesus' private conversation with the disciples) that Jesus will arbitrate between himself and his brother. This leads to the discourse on wealth which Matthew has inserted into the Sermon on the Mount; it has been seen above (p. 29) that this section (13–34) bears traces of the time when it was simply a collection of sayings each introduced with 'and he said' or a similar formula. The collection ends well with the striking phrase of verse 34. What follows is really concerned not with the correct attitude towards worldly riches but with the duty of watchfulness in view of the imminence of the Second Coming; it is only in the allusion to the thief in the night at 39 and in the language of 45 f. that we get any kind of association between the sayings on worldly riches and these verses. But these slight resemblances are merely fortuitous; from xii. 35–48 we have a single coherent homily on watchfulness; Peter's question appears to have been introduced to make it clear that the charge is delivered primarily to the disciples as rulers of the Church, and is probably a Lucan addition (see Creed, *ad loc.*). The remainder of the chapter may be derived from a different collection of sayings, but continues to deal with the subject of the imminent return of the Lord and concludes well with the warning of xii. 59.[1]

It is no doubt possible that Luke has simply inserted the collection of sayings on worldly riches into a collection on boldness in preaching which led up to the general homily on watchfulness of xii. 35–9. But there seems no reason why he should have done so and in general he copies his sources faithfully, except in a few cases (see below, p. 85) where he seems to have inserted a piece of narrative into a discourse, apparently in order to break the monotony of too long a series of sayings.

Thus it seems safer to suppose that the sayings on watchfulness had no original connexion with the preceding parts of the chapter, but are simply an independent collection, added here by Luke because the eschatological note in verses 31–4 leads on to the sermon on watchfulness. (It is of course possible that the connexion is due to the combination of two tracts by an earlier compiler.)

Thus it seems likely that we may have three collections of sayings. The conflation of the first two collections might be thought apparent in the confusion which is felt in the double introduction, xi. 53–xii. 1. But the tentative possibility has already been noted that the Lucan

---

[1] For some of the problems arising out of Luke xii. 35–59 cf. below, p. 70.

ending to the denunciation of the Pharisees and lawyers (xi. 53–4) may preserve an original element of the source, marking the transition to the Passion narrative (see Vol. I, pp. 101–2). The suggestion is perhaps strengthened by the following saying concerning the leaven of the Pharisees. Mark has the saying at viii. 15, which falls in Luke's 'great omission'. But the Marcan context has little verisimilitude. The saying naturally belongs to a late stage of the ministry, and was originally a warning against *agents provocateurs* who might entrap the disciples into fatal indiscretions (see Vol. I, p. 57). This warning also, therefore, may have stood at the transition in the source containing the denunciation of the Pharisees. This is not to say that the wording has not been written up by Luke; in xi. 53–4 we have the classical ἐνεδρεύειν and θηρεῦσαι and the even more interesting ἀποστοματίζειν (cf. Vol. I, p. 102, n. 1). It is hard to be confident whether the milling crowd of xii. 1 was mentioned in this source, or whether (as is perhaps more probable) it is inserted here by Luke, in order to make an adequate join to his next section, xii. 2–12, consisting of sayings originally addressed to the multitude, though the presence of the private warning to the disciples in xii. 1 remains awkward, and suggests that the join was not over-skilfully made.

Luke xii. 13–34 thus falls out as a completely independent collection with an opening narrative of a request put to Jesus by one of the multitude, which in such sources is conventionally assumed to be present and listening at any given moment. It is not impossible that the mention of the multitude may have suggested to Luke the insertion of the tract at this point, since he already had the multitude from xii. 1 and no doubt felt it necessary to make some use of them. The collection manifests the character of a primitive collection, since we have two further introductory phrases at 15 and 22, and also at 16 to introduce the parable of the rich fool. This parable (xii. 16–21) does not appear at all in Matthew and shows signs of Lucan rewriting,[1] while the rabbinical use of the third person plural as meaning 'God'

---

[1] Luke xii. 16 b has admirably compressed syntax, comparable to the rewriting evident at Luke vii. 2; note also the tetracolon with asyndeton and chiasmus in the received text of 19. This is omitted in D and the Old Latin, and Creed is inclined to follow Wellhausen and Blass in omitting κείμενα εἰς ἔτη πολλά· ἀναπαύου, φάγε, πίε, with these manuscripts. It is grossly improbable that a copyist could have written such excellent rhetorical Greek in a thoroughly Lucan style (cf. Luke xvii. 27).

appears to be a mark of a peculiar Lucan stratum of tradition (cf. my *Hellenistic Elements*, p. 9), though it cannot be attributed to Luke himself who would hardly have understood the Semitic periphrasis and certainly would never have coined it out of his own head. The question is whether the parable was an original part of the collection. In the sayings of Luke xii. 22 ff. the degree of verbal identity with Matthew (vi. 25 ff.) is high; and it is striking that Matthew, immediately preceding all this at vi. 24, has the saying 'No man can serve two masters . . . ye cannot serve God and Mammon', which Luke has in a quite different position, attached to the sequel to the parable of the unjust steward (xvi. 13). It looks as if Luke had the parable of the rich fool at his disposal, and inserted it at this point to replace 'Ye cannot serve God and Mammon', which accordingly had to be transferred to the next context at which it would seem appropriate (cf. pp. 29, 95). But otherwise the original collection seems to have been incorporated without much revision. There is of course little connexion between the refusal of Jesus to arbitrate (xii. 13–14) and the ensuing warnings against covetousness, and Creed (pp. 172–3) suggests that the joining of them is 'to be ascribed to the evangelist rather than to tradition'. It is certainly likely enough that there was no original connexion whatever between the refusal to arbitrate and the warnings which in any event show every sign of having been isolated sayings. Nevertheless it may well have been there in the pre-Lucan collection since we otherwise father on Luke the intolerably clumsy Greek of τινì...αὐτοῦ...αὐτῷ in 15 which looks suspiciously like an editorial connexion, intended to link the refusal of arbitration with the following sayings.

'Fear not little flock' in Luke xii. 32 is omitted by Matthew from the Sermon on the Mount, perhaps because he thought its intimacy unsuited to the solemn proclamation of the new Torah from the new Sinai. On the other hand, xii. 33–4 seems to have been remodelled by Luke (cf. Creed *ad loc.*), perhaps to provide a transition from the gnomic wisdom[1] of 22–31 to the apocalyptic style of 35 ff. It remains possible that even though Matthew has preserved the original form of the saying about 'treasures in heaven', Luke has kept its original position at the end of the collection. But if so Matthew's ending of

---

[1] Cf. Windisch, *Der Sinn der Bergpredigt*, pp. 20 ff., for this collection of sayings as having the characteristics of 'Wisdom-literature'.

this section of the Sermon on the Mount at vi. 34 ('The morrow will take care of itself; sufficient unto the day is the evil thereof') must have been an unattached saying for which the evangelist found a singularly appropriate position.

The section that follows (Luke xii. 35–59) is probably again a composite structure. The first part (35–49) is a well-marked unit, though with no formal narrative introduction of the ordinary kind. On the other hand such introductions, while they may be of considerable length, as at Luke xiii. 1 and xv. 1, may in the first instance have amounted in some cases to no more than 'And he said unto his disciples' or some such phrase which could simply be eliminated.

The collection itself presents some remarkable features. The sayings of Luke xii. 42–6 (= Matt. xxiv. 45–51) seem to have come to Luke and Matthew in an identical form; the only notable changes are that the faithful slave of Matt. xxiv. 45 becomes a steward in Luke xii. 42, though he reverts to servile rank in 43. But in 42 he is in charge of a 'retinue' of servants, rather than a mere 'household' of slaves, and it is his duty to dispense a σιτομέτριον rather than to give them their food. It looks as though this is another of the instances where Luke improves the social status on account of the circles for which the Gospel was intended; of course the steward of an important household might be a slave, but the reversion in 43 suggests that the verse is already a popular text of Christian homiletic. Again in 45 he rises in the scale; he has under him both menservants and maids, not merely fellow-slaves as in Matt. xxiv. 49. The other variations are no more than stylistic, while the wording of Luke xii. 46 and Matt. xxiv. 50–51 a is exact, except for the substitution of hypocrites for unbelievers by Matthew, who presumably has orthodox Jews of the Pharisaic type in his mind. Both have the rare διχοτομήσει.

The tradition at the back of Luke xii. 35–7 is extremely complex. Matthew does not reproduce the verses, having the equivalent in the parable of the wise and foolish virgins; moreover, they have a close parallel in Mark xiii. 33–7. It looks as if Luke incorporates a fragmentary reminiscence of Mark and of Matthew's parable. The linguistic evidence (ἐλθόντος...κρούσαντος...αὐτῷ) is decisive against the view that Luke himself is responsible for watering down the parable into the teaching of xii. 36. The verb γρηγορεῖν is noted

by Phrynichus as non-Attic, and is only found in Luke in this passage (37 and 39); moreover, we have here one of Luke's failures to
correct the barbarous ἀμήν of his sources, though a few verses later
(44) he has corrected the ἀμήν of Matt. xxiv. 47 into ἀληθῶς. We have
therefore fairly clear evidence that the passage is pre-Lucan. In the
source that Luke used the sayings had already been subjected to
some allegorizing tendencies (cf. 37b), just as in different ways the
same phenomenon is apparent in Matthew's parable (xxv. 5 χρονί-
ζοντος τοῦ νυμφίου, and 11 f.), where this is even more prominent.
But it is highly improbable that Luke's sayings do not ultimately
go back to an original parable of Jesus, a developed and allegorized
form of which is preserved in Matthew. In Luke's source the
parable had been lost, and had become a piece of parabolic teaching.
Once again we have to allow for a very complicated development
of the tradition.

At Luke xii. 41 we have a typical interruption in Peter's question
as to whether the parable applies to all Christians or to the disciples
only. The question is not in Matthew; but the answer of Jesus
(Matt. xxiv. 45) opens with the same phrase (τίς ἄρα) as in Luke.
The phrase seems slightly more appropriate in its Lucan position
as an answer to a question, though possible in the Matthean; it is
quite likely that originally the saying stood as a separate item in a
series of sayings with this introduction, following an 'and he said',
and that the words suggested to Luke the appropriateness of a
question at this point. On the other hand it must be recognized that
if Peter's question is inserted by Luke in order to make it clear that
the warnings of the preceding verses are addressed primarily to the
disciples as rulers of the Church, while in fact they were originally,
in so far as they are authentic, addressed to all disciples, the insertion
is not very effective. It is true that the substitution of οἰκονόμος or
δοῦλος in 42 and of the men-servants and maid-servants for the
'fellow-servants' seems to limit the application to those who are in
some position of authority; but xii. 47 and 48, which do not appear
in Matthew, weaken the effect by making the warnings refer to all
servants alike, though the more responsible servant will be punished
more severely. It is curious that Luke, if he inserted the question of
Peter, should have added these verses here, as Creed (p. 177) seems
to imply. I am inclined to suggest that the question of Peter was

part of the tradition as known to both Matthew and Luke, though probably it was not inserted into the collection of sayings until a regular Christian ministry began to develop, and that xii. 47 and 48 represent a Lucan expansion to make it clear that the warning to vigilance applies in fact to all Christians, though pre-eminently to those holding some pastoral office. Matthew has to a certain extent achieved the same result by eliminating Peter's question. But this can be no more than a conjecture.

With Luke xii. 49 the style changes abruptly. In place of the reasoned, homiletic style of the preceding verses we have a collection of isolated sayings connected by a general reference to the Parousia, but with no logical sequence of thought. The sayings in themselves have a high claim to authenticity as isolated fragments of the words of Jesus, which survived even though not understood. The saying (or sayings?) of 49–50 seems to be drawn from a prediction of the Passion; the word βαπτίζειν is used by Josephus of overwhelming with troubles (*B.J.* IV, 137), but Oepke[1] holds that the use of טבל and βαπτίζειν in this sense is not genuinely Jewish, and that an original saying in which Jesus foretold his death, in language based on the metaphorical usage of being overwhelmed by the flood of disaster (Ps. xlii. 8, lxix. 2, etc.), has been transposed into the language of baptism under the influence of the Hellenistic Church. But *Pap. Par.* XLVII, 13, κἂν ἴδῃς ὅτι μέλλομεν σωθῆναι, τότε βαπτιζώμεθα,[2] shows that this use was to be found among quite uneducated people; it would seem that the original saying was simply a prediction of a 'baptism' of being overwhelmed by calamities, but that it has been expanded under Christian influence into 'being baptized with a baptism'; the expansion may have been suggested by a reminiscence of the Baptist's prophecy that Jesus would bring a baptism of fire.

The saying of Luke xii. 51ff. looks more original in its Matthean form; Matthew is nearer than Luke to the prophecy of Mic. vii. 6 and 'sword' seems preferable to the abstract 'division'.[3]

Matthew's use of the material is instructive. The tract on boldness in preaching (Luke xii. 2–12) appears in his expanded charge to the Twelve (Matt. x. 26 ff. and 19 ff.) except for Luke xii. 10 which

[1] *T.W.z.N.T.* 1, 534 and 536.
[2] Quoted in Moulton and Milligan, *Voc.Gr.N.T.* s.v.
[3] For the whole text cf. Dodd, *Parables of the Kingdom*, p. 68.

is omitted here, and transferred to Matt. xii. 32 to take the place of
Mark iii. 28 f. The next section on riches appears bodily in the
Sermon on the Mount (Matt. vi. 26 ff.), except for the opening
request and the parable of the rich fool (cf. above, p. 29). The
section Luke xii. 35–49 has been incorporated into the Marcan apocalypse (Matt. xxiv. 42 ff.), except that 35–8 are omitted presumably
as being covered by the parable of the ten virgins, though the striking
verse 37 disappears; 47 and 48 do not appear, but have already been
noted as probably a Lucan insertion. Verses 49 and 50 do not appear,
while 51–3 are transferred to Matt. x. 34.

This grouping by Matthew is of course compatible with the view
that his material came to him as part of a single document, which
Luke has preserved in its original sequence; it is certainly not compatible with the view that Luke's arrangement of his material is his
own handiwork, since it presents a hopeless confusion. It is, on the
other hand, more probable that Matthew and Luke both had before
them one short written source containing Luke xii. 2–12, a second
(probably) containing Luke xii. 13–34 (without the parable of the
rich fool?), and a third containing Luke xiii. 24–46. Apart from these
three blocks of homogeneous material, which Luke has preserved
while Matthew has broken them up and omitted what he could not
use or did not need, the rest (Luke xii. 47–end) consists of a Lucan
homiletic expansion and a block of isolated sayings.[1]

---

[1] For Luke xii. 57–9 cf. above, p. 20.

CHAPTER IX

THE NATIONALIST PERIL

Following the isolated sayings of Luke xii. 49–53, the next distinguishable section of Luke would seem to run from xii. 54 to xiii. 9. Creed (p. 180) rightly sees that the theme of the closing verses of Luke xii is carried on in what follows. But he fails to do justice to the meaning; the section is not simply a warning of the coming judgement, but a warning of the dangers that await the nation if they follow the lead of those who are trying to force them into rebellion against Rome. In 54–6 it is very hard to attach any meaning to the signs of the times. They might indeed be drawn from the 'realized eschatology' of the teaching of Jesus, but in that case we should expect to find the lesson drawn from something already happening, such as the budding of the fig-tree in Mark xiii. 28, not from the future as in the weather forecast. The sayings of 57 ff. are even more difficult. xii. 57 may be an editorial insertion by Luke, replacing an original 'and he said'; the change from the plural to the singular in 58 suggests that originally the two sets of sayings were uttered on different occasions, while it is hard to see what the reference to τὸ δίκαιον means. The view that they were originally separate is supported by Matthew; he has included the saying in the Sermon on the Mount (v. 25 f.), though the difference of wording is such that it is not necessary to suppose that he is drawing on the same written source as Luke. It is possible that the changes are simply due to compression by Matthew; Luke's version is nearer the original with a good parallelism at the end of 58 and the vivid πράκτωρ as against the colourless ὑπηρέτης. The closing sentence is practically identical, Luke having changed κοδράντης into λεπτόν to avoid the barbarism; but here we are dealing with an epigrammatic saying which would naturally retain its original form in any line of transmission.

On any showing the Matthean position is purely artificial; Matthew has chosen to interpret the saying as referring to a state of punishment after death and attached it to the warning of hell-fire with which his source for the new Torah ended (at v. 22, cf. above, p. 20). But the interpretation of the adversary in the Matthean context is extremely difficult; apparently he is an injured brother, 'the judge' presumably being God, and 'the officer' the devil or an angel of punishment; but all this is left to the reader's imagination.

On the other hand, if we suppose that these two sayings form part of a tract from which the opening of Luke xiii is also drawn, we get a perfectly clear meaning. The hearers are to judge of the danger of 'this time' as they would judge of the weather; they are to have the good sense to reconcile themselves to the Roman government, before it is too late and they find themselves in the position of the loser of a lawsuit in which the winner will be entirely merciless. It may be noted in favour of this explanation that the meaning of the saying was lost at a very early date. (It is quite possible that Luke did not understand it.) Matthew may not have known it, or he may have found it unintelligible. But the saying circulated in an entirely different wording, and was still known after the completion of Matthew, into which it has been inserted by an early copyist (xvi. 2 f.).[1]

The opening verses of Luke xiii suit this interpretation exactly. Nothing is known of the Galileans or the tower of Siloam. Josephus' source for this period loses no opportunity of blackening Pilate's character.[2] But the massacre of a few Galileans during a riot at the Passover or some similar occasion might well be too small a matter to excite any particular interest, especially if they belonged to the disaffected element in the population which Josephus habitually writes off as brigands; moreover his source for this period, as used both in the *Antiquities* and in the *Jewish War*, is grossly inadequate. Naturally the fall of the tower of Siloam would scarcely merit his attention. In any case his source for this period both in the *War* and the *Antiquities* contained nothing but a few incidents from the history of Judaea. There is no reason for supposing that Luke's source here

---

[1] Cf. Streeter, *The Four Gospels*, p. 241.

[2] Cf. his treatment of the incident of the water-supply in *B.J.* II, 175 ff. For Josephus' source at this point cf. Hölscher in *P.W.K.* IX, 1948 and 1988 ff. Schlatter, *Gesch. Israels v. Alex. d. Gr. bis Hadrian*, p. 277, suggests a collection of anecdotes intended to show that the blame for the Jewish rebellion rests on the procurators (perhaps rightly—cf. Tacitus, *Hist.* v, 10: 'Duravit tamen patientia Iudaeis usque ad Gessium Florum procuratorem: sub eo bellum ortum').

has not preserved an authentic record of a forgotten incident, trivial to the historian but sensational in its importance to the people of Galilee at the period. The omission of the story in Matthew is not surprising; the massacre was trifling, and the saying of the Lord not of any particular value to the early Church, which knew perfectly well that the Jews had 'perished' because they had refused to repent. Luke has preserved it because he normally preserves his sources as entities; the Semitic origin of the story stands out in the ὧν ... αὐτῶν of xiii. 1 and the ἐφ' οὓς ... αὐτούς of v. 4.[1] It might indeed be argued that in the latter verse αὐτούς is needed as an object for ἀπέκτεινεν, but Luke could perfectly well have omitted ἀπέκτεινεν leaving it to the reader to understand that the fall of the tower had the fatal effects which would naturally be expected. The incidents referred to throw an interesting light on the duration and circumstances of Jesus' ministry in Galilee. In the Lucan narrative they occur while Jesus is on his last journey to Jerusalem, but this setting is of course fictitious. The natural occasion for such an incident would be one of the three great festivals, Passover, Weeks or Tabernacles, when there were large crowds of Galileans in Jerusalem, and a disturbance would easily arise which might lead to the massacre. We cannot rule out the possibility of a disturbance at the feast of Tabernacles;[2] but it seems doubtful whether it was attended by large crowds of pilgrims, as the Passover was.[3] It would seem that the purpose of those who brought the message was to force Jesus, who had already attracted attention as the leader of a new religious movement, into showing his hand in regard to the Roman government in view of Pilate's latest outrage; his reply is simply a call to repentance. It would seem that we must allow for a period of teaching long enough

---

[1] ὀφειλέτης in 4 as = ἁμαρτωλός is also an Aramaism (so Grimm-Thayer, s.v.; L.S.J. and Voc.Gr.N.T. give no parallels). Cf. M. Black, *An Aramaic Approach to the Gospels and Acts*[2] (1954), p. 102.

[2] For the festivals as likely occasions of disturbance cf. Vol. I, p. 118, and for a disturbance at the feast of Tabernacles *Antt.* XIII, 372 (from a Jewish reviser who has falsified Nicolaus of Damascus to suit his own tendency; cf. Hölscher in *P.W.K.* IX, 1983).

[3] The command to dwell in booths could be observed anywhere; the main feature of the solemnity was the illumination of the Temple on the first day of the feast (the water-drawing was repeated daily for the seven days of the feast); Moore doubts whether it was largely attended by pilgrims from a distance (*Judaism*, II, 49).

to draw attention at least before the feast of Tabernacles, and more probably before the Passover preceding the Crucifixion.

The source concluded, so far as we can say, with the parable of the fig tree, again a warning of the danger of the rejection of the Jewish nation. Matthew has omitted it because he has the miracle of the fig tree in its Marcan position; but the parable is the original.[1]

[1] For the parable cf. my *Hellenistic Elements*, p. 19.

CHAPTER X

A COLLECTION OF FRAGMENTS

After the parable of the fig tree, the rest of Luke xiii is a very miscellaneous collection. The story of xiii. 10–17 may be a miracle-story developed out of a pronouncement-story of the same type as xiv. 1 ff.[1] If so, however, it is not Luke but a predecessor who is responsible; the passage is marked by some very non-Lucan Greek in ἰδού and the periphrastic imperfects in 10 and 11; this is common enough in Luke where he is following a source, but is not found in the latter half of Acts, except where it is justified by the sense, or where, as in Acts xxii. 19, he is professing to report a speech delivered by Paul in Aramaic.[2] It is possible that xiii. 10–13 came to him as a conventional miracle-story (in spite of its brevity it has all the features of such a story, the details which show that the case was genuine and serious in 11, the word of power and healing act in 13, leading on to the cure and an acclamation by the patient); and Luke may have added the dialogue with the ruler of the synagogue, which is a variant of xiv. 5 (=Matt. xii. 11). But the difficulty of such a view is that the dialogue could not have existed without a miracle of healing on the Sabbath to introduce it; further, although the glorification of God by the patient would serve as an acclamation, yet ν. 17 is virtually necessary as the conclusion of the whole affair. It may well be asked whether we have not here an early miracle-story, which has not travelled far enough in the tradition to be adapted to the proper 'form'.

The two parables which follow (xiii. 18–21) may have come to Luke with the sayings of xiii. 22–30 as a tract dealing with the kingdom of God; the fact that the sayings deal with the kingdom as a

---

[1] So apparently Dibelius, *Formgeschichte d. Evang.*², p. 94 (Eng. trans. p. 97).
[2] Cf. Blass-Debrunner, *N.T. Grammatik* §353. 3 (esp. appendix, 7th ed., p. 58). Note σάββασιν in Luke xiii. 10. The plural (without ἡ ἡμέρα τῶν...) occurs five times in Mark, and also in Matt. xii. 5, 10, 11 and 12. Luke preserves the plural at iv. 31 (=Mark i. 21) and vi. 2 (=Mark ii. 24). In vi. 1 (=Mark ii. 23), 7 (=Mark iii. 2) and 9 (=Mark iii. 4), and at xiv. 3 (=Matt. xii. 10 ff.) he has altered it to the singular. Clearly, where he retains it, he has forgotten to revise his source.

gradual process of growth, while the following group looks forward to it as a catastrophic event, is no necessary argument against the view that they were grouped together in a single collection; they are not united by the common theme of the kingdom of God, and it would not matter to the compiler that the kingdom of God meant something different in different sayings.[1] It would seem that the parable of the mustard seed originally circulated in two forms, the Marcan and the Lucan; Matthew's version is simply a conflation of the two, which shows that he had both forms of the parable before him.[2] The fortunate fact that Luke has omitted to correct the barbarous σάτα (= the Jewish *seah*, found only here in the New Testament) gives us a complete verbal identity for the two versions of the leaven. Whether they were an original pair is another matter (cf. Smith, pp. 40 f.).

This identity of the two parables in the Q form is in marked contrast with the following section. We have a purely Lucan introduction at xiii. 22 which fits a collection of sayings into the supposed journey to Jerusalem; the sayings all have counterparts in Matthew, though the similarity of wording is never enough to make it certain whether the evangelists are using a common written source or drawing on two parallel lines of tradition. Thus in the saying about the narrow gate in Luke xiii. 24 the only significant words which appear in Matt. vii. 13 f. are εἰσελθεῖν (εἰσέλθατε) and στενή. On the other hand Matthew has a fine Semitic parallelism which is probably original; Luke did not appreciate it, and the differences of wording may merely be due to his drastic abbreviations. xiii. 25 is sub-

[1] As they stand in Luke the parables seem to refer to the gradual growth of the kingdom, i.e. the Church; whether this was the original intention is another matter. For the original meaning cf. Dodd, *Parables of the Kingdom*, pp. 189 ff. The Marcan insertion of the smallness of the grain of mustard seed, though it does not appear in the Q version, seems to give the key to the meaning as understood by the compiler who joined it to the leaven, though the original meaning was that the branches of the 'mustard-tree' are now available for all men and that the kingdom which has hitherto been working in secret is now showing its fulfilment in the ministry of Jesus.

[2] It is of course possible that the formal introduction of Luke xiii. 18 has been transferred by Luke from Mark iv. 30 to introduce the version of the parable which came to him in his other source. This, however, seems most unlikely; so short a parable would not naturally demand an introduction of this kind, when the Prodigal Son can be introduced by a simple 'And he said'. It would seem that both versions go back to a period of the tradition when the parables circulated with this kind of introduction, but had not yet been collected into larger groups.

stantially the same as the conclusion of the parable of the ten virgins (= Matt. xxv. 11 f.); the similarity of wording is close (though the nature of the saying would hardly allow of much difference), and the sudden appearance of the master of the house, and the change from a narrow door which it is hard to enter to a door which you must enter at once before it is shut, show that we are dealing with a faint reminiscence of a parable, the rest of which has been forgotten. Thus we have no reason for supposing that Matthew did not have the saying before him in his source; he would naturally omit it, if it also occurred in a more impressive form in the source from which he drew the parable of the ten virgins. It seems that the parable was preserved in one line of tradition, while it dwindled into a mere reminiscence in the other.

The probability that Luke is using an older collection of sayings is strengthened by the good connexion between xiii. 25 and 26. Here the Lucan version may be a stage nearer to the original: it is a warning to the Jewish nation of the danger of rejection. Matthew has rewritten it and transferred it to the closing warning against false prophets in the Sermon on the Mount (vii. 22 ff.), where it appears that since they are false prophets, they have to have miracles to their credit. The warning to the Jewish nation that they cannot claim preference because Jesus lived among them is clearly original, while the closing warning of Luke xiii. 28 and Matt. vii. 23 shows, in spite of its curious verbal differences, that both are using the same source[1] for 26 f., and makes it probable that this source began at 24.

The warning is continued (Luke xiii. 28) with the saying concerning the patriarchs in the kingdom of God; it is to be presumed that this came to Luke with the 'weeping and gnashing of teeth', a favourite Matthean theme not found elsewhere in the Gospels except in this Lucan saying. Its presence here suggests that Matthew has drawn on the same source for his insertion of the patriarchs into the story of the centurion's servant (viii. 11 f.). The apocalyptic picture would hardly suit the Sermon on the Mount, while it fits in admirably in its present Matthean position; it is quite possible that his sole reason for inserting it there was that he wanted to get rid of it as soon as possible after the Sermon in order not to have a small fragment left on his hands. The last sentence, Luke xiii. 30, probably belonged

[1] For the variations in the citation of Ps. vi. 9 cf. above, p. 32.

to the source: Matthew omits it after viii. 12 since it was one of those proverbial sayings which could be inserted at any appropriate position. Moreover, he was using it at xix. 30 in its Marcan context (Mark x. 31).

Thus on the whole the evidence suggests that at least Luke xiii. 23–30, and quite possibly the two parables which precede it, formed a collection of sayings dealing with the kingdom of God. The opening of verse 18 is hopelessly abrupt, and looks as though it was a continuation of a series of sayings which originally had a more formal narrative opening. This is of course quite possible; there may have been one or more parables of the same kind in the original source, which Luke has omitted because they were duplicates of parables which he has inserted elsewhere from some other collection. In any case the clumsiness at this point can hardly be due to anything but a passage from one source to another, which Luke has not taken the trouble to smoothe over.[1]

At xiii. 31 Luke inserts a detached episode which, as Creed points out, really belongs to an earlier stage in the history, during the ministry of Jesus in Galilee and not on a journey to Jerusalem when he is *ex hypothesi* already departing out of Antipas' territories, if he is not out of them already. But it is certainly historical; it is entirely contrary to the tendency of the later Church to suppose that the Pharisees would give Jesus a friendly warning.[2] Jesus'

---

[1] It is no doubt possible that the collection simply began ἔλεγεν ὁ Ἰησοῦς and that Luke omitted the name of Jesus as sufficiently implied by the fact that he was the speaker in 18. This would explain the lack of a more formal opening; but the abruptness still betrays a clumsy compilation of sources.

[2] Dibelius (*Formgesch. d. Evang.*², pp. 162–3, Eng. trans. pp. 162–3) regards this view, which is also that of Goguel (*Vie de Jésus*, pp. 333 f.), as doubtful; he thinks that here the Pharisees were inserted into the story by Luke as being the usual opposition to Jesus (as in xvi. 14 and xvii. 20), and that the improbability of such opponents giving him a friendly warning never crossed Luke's mind; any of Jesus' dialogues not held with disciples must have been held with Pharisees. But it is extremely doubtful whether the evangelist went to work in this kind of way. At xvi. 14 the Pharisees mock, as conventional opponents; there is no real parallel here. And at xvii. 20 the fact that Luke has rewritten the introduction of the saying offers no ground for supposing that he invented the saying or the identity of the questioners, since he is quite liable to redraft the wording of his sources, as at vii. 2. And it appears tenuous argument to suppose with Dibelius that the appearance of Herod here is due to Luke's interest in the great ones of the earth. His view may rank among the curiosities of form-criticism. For the meaning of fox cf. Creed *ad loc.*

answer as it stands appears quite unintelligible; Creed, following Wellhausen, is probably right in supposing that the original answer was ἰδοὺ ἐκβάλλω ... αὔριον· πλὴν δεῖ με τῇ ἐχομένῃ πορεύεσθαι κτλ., and that καὶ τῇ τρίτῃ τελειοῦμαι was a gloss to introduce the Crucifixion and Resurrection. The second σήμερον καὶ αὔριον καί then became necessary to introduce the τῇ ἐχομένῃ. It should be observed that this view is much easier to accept if the 'primitive corruption' had found its way into the saying before it reached Luke.

The reply to Herod furnishes an excellent introduction to the lament over Jerusalem (Luke xiii. 34). Whether the opening implies previous visits of Jesus to the city, at which he had failed to win the following he had hoped for, or simply that he had often thought of coming, but decided that there was no chance of gaining a hearing, cannot be said; the words could bear either meaning and cannot be used as an argument in favour of the view that the Synoptic tradition has failed to record other visits. It would seem that the exalted prophetic style of the saying caused its preservation in identical words as an unattached saying; Matthew inserts it as the conclusion of his denunciation of the scribes and Pharisees. Here too the situation is eminently suitable for the actual lament over Jerusalem, though the position is simply due to Matthew. Unfortunately in neither case does the situation suit the closing saying of Luke xiii. 35 (= Matt. xxiii. 39). In Luke, as it stands, it could only mean 'You shall not see me until my triumphal entry' (xix. 38). As Creed points out, this gives a bald sense and a poor connexion; the triumphal entry is presumably only a few days off. In the Matthean position it presumably means 'Until you greet me when I return in glory'; Jesus is already in Jerusalem for the last time. It seems unlikely that the words are a Messianic addition by the Church; for Jerusalem was never expected to have the chance of welcoming Jesus as the Messiah until his final return, when he would presumably not come to Jerusalem at all. The probability is that the saying of Luke xiii. 35 always formed part of the lament over Jerusalem, and that the whole belongs to an early stage in the ministry of Jesus, when he had hoped to go up to Jerusalem, but had reason to believe that he would not find a hearing; it will mean 'I will not visit you until you are prepared to receive me as coming in the name of the Lord', a decision which was later altered into the decision to go up and face rejection.

It is remarkable that the chapter begins and ends with incidents which appear to preserve good historical reminiscences of the relations of Jesus with the outer world of the nationalist movement and Herod Antipas, which is striking in view of the general lack of reference of this sort in the general Gospel tradition. But it is probably a mere coincidence that they come so close together in the Lucan narrative. It must further be noted that even if the section xiii. 18–30 is part of an older collection of sayings, it is scarcely more than a part; and it is impossible to be certain that the two parables of 18–21 belong to that collection. They may simply have come to Luke independently. Thus it is possible that the whole chapter from verse 10 to the end is a collection of fragments which Luke has inserted here for no particular reason; they were in his tradition, and had to be put in somewhere.[1]

[1] The identity of the lament over Jerusalem in Matt. xxiii. 37–9 and Luke xiii. 34–5 is exact, unless the strongly supported ἔρημος of Matthew is correct, as it probably is; it is more likely to have been omitted by assimilation to Luke than inserted into Matthew. It is an apparently unconnected saying which has come down practically unchanged, though there is no indication of a written source common to the evangelists. It is of course possible that Luke xiii. 31 ff. is a fragment of such a source, the rest of which Luke has not used; but it is more likely that the prophetic form of the saying and its importance as a warning of the coming doom of the city led to its preservation in an identical form in oral tradition.

CHAPTER XI

BANQUET SAYINGS

Luke xiv. 1–24 contains another collection of sayings with a well-marked, though entirely mechanical, unity: all have something to do with banquets. The narrative introduction is of interest. It has probably been added by Luke at this point merely because the setting was at a meal with a Pharisee.[1] On the other hand the construction καὶ ἐγένετο καί, usually with αὐτός or αὐτοί after it, although common in the Gospel, is only once (and doubtfully) found in Acts (cf. Creed on Luke i. 8). Further the double αὐτός and αὐτόν and the periphrastic conjugation (the similar incident of Mark iii. 2 has the better παρετήρουν) indicate that Luke has inserted the story as it came to him. But it has no real connexion with what follows, and it is at least doubtful whether the invitation of the Pharisee is compatible with the deliberate attempt to find an opening for attacking Jesus. The story took its present form when the Pharisees were conventional villains, but before it reached Luke. The pronouncement which is the point of the story appears in Matthew in the entirely different setting of the healing of the man with the withered hand (Matt. xii. 9 ff.=Mark iii. 1 ff.), where it displaces the question 'Is it lawful to do good or to do evil on the sabbath-day?'. It seems that Matthew inserts the question there because he had lost the clue to the meaning of that somewhat cryptic saying (cf. Vol. 1, p. 11). On the other hand there is no conclusive evidence that Matthew is using the same source as Luke for the saying; the verbal identity is confined to the non-significant words.[2] It is of course possible that there were several healings on the Sabbath which led to a similar argument; there are three in the Lucan tradition (vi. 6 ff., xiii. 1 ff. and here). But it is to be presumed that, while the tradition has preserved a general memory of miracles of healing and the pronouncement on the Sabbath, the association of the saying with a particular incident is due to the evangelists or their sources. Matthew

---

[1] So Creed rightly suggests, *ad loc.*

[2] For the unsolved problem of the reading in Luke xiv. 5 cf. Creed *ad loc.* The 'sheep' of D is obviously an attempt at emendation based on Matt. xii. 11.

has inserted the Lucan argument with the Pharisees into the Marcan story; there is no evidence to show whether it came to him from one or other of Luke's sources or not.

Whether Luke has inserted the healing into a collection of sayings, or whether it came to him already united to the rest of the material of xiv. 1–24 is uncertain. It would seem that the motive for the insertion of the story at this point was to avoid the monotony of an unbroken series of sayings; this consideration might apply to the primitive evangelist addressing a congregation more than to Luke. On the other hand the difficulties pointed out by Creed, that the language of verse 8 is general and inappropriate to the guests who are choosing their seats at the moment, and that 12 is 'equally inappropriate, if spoken to an actual host whose hospitality has been accepted', can equally well be explained as due either to the artlessness of the primitive compiler of the tract (the Pharisees can always be treated with a complete lack of courtesy, except in a few cases which go back beyond the general convention of the Gospels), or to Luke's carelessness in inserting his story into a source which simply told how Jesus went into the house of a Pharisee to eat bread and uttered the sayings of 8–24. On this view the inappropriateness of verse 7 will be due to Luke, who presumably felt that some transition from the pronouncement-story to the sayings on behaviour at dinner was needed, but failed to notice that the general saying hardly suited the particular situation. It is not unreasonable to suppose that the fault is due to the original compiler of the tract or perhaps to a clumsy reviser who inserted the miracle before the whole came to Luke; but Luke himself is quite capable of this sort of carelessness.

The collection of sayings in itself is marked by a strikingly Semitic excess in the matter of pronouns representing the Semitic suffix (note the wholly unnecessary use of the second person singular in 10 and 12). It appears to have been unknown to Matthew. Verse 11 is a floating saying which might come anywhere in the tradition, and it is possible that its insertion here is due to Luke, though more probably it stood in his sources here and at xviii. 14. This is the only saying common to Luke and Matthew until we come to the parable of the unwilling guests. Here the verbal resemblances between Matt. xxii. 3 ff. and Luke xiv. 16 ff. are at a minimum, and it is quite unsafe to suppose that Matthew and Luke are drawing on the same source, especially as Luke has a good Semitic parallelism in 18 ff., which is not to be found in Matthew. The murder of the servants, and the guest without a wedding garment (possibly once an independent parable),[1] may be due to Matthew, but it is quite possible that they had found their way into the parable before it reached him. The interruption which leads up to the parable probably stood in Luke's source, since we should expect an interruption at this point. It may be a Lucan interpolation, but there seems no adequate reason for supposing that this is the case.

The rest of Luke xiv probably comes from a different source. The section, or part of it, might have been appended to the parable of the unwilling guests as a corrective to a possible misunderstanding of the parable; Jesus calls the poor and outcast, but he calls them to the bearing of the cross. This would provide the same kind of corrective as Matthew's man without a wedding garment. But this is unlikely. The banquet source seems to have been compiled on a principle of mechanical association; all the sayings have something to do with banquets. On the other hand while there is no evidence that Matthew knew any of the banquet-sayings, it is clear that he knew the sayings of verses 26 and 27 in a form closely resembling the Lucan, and also nearer to the original. The threefold parallelism of Matt. x. 37 f. ('he that loveth . . . , he that loveth . . . , he that taketh not . . .') leading up in each case to 'is not worthy of me', followed by the double parallelism of the widely current saying of Matt. x. 39, looks more original than Luke's somewhat clumsy combination of the various relations whom a man must be prepared to 'hate' into a single clause with an attempt at an exhaustive enumeration of all possible relatives. Still more suspicious is his insertion of 'and moreover his own soul also', which looks like a compression of the thought of Matt. x. 39 into a single subordinate clause, perhaps to be explained by the fact that Luke has already dealt with the theme at ix. 23 (=Mark iv. 35) and has another version of it coming at xvii. 33. The problem is complicated by the fact that Luke xiv. 34 and 35 are also known to Matthew in a form resembling the Lucan. In the Marcan tradition it has lost its context and meaning (Vol. I, p. 67); in Matthew and Luke it is applied to the disciples as 'the salt of the earth'. The wording in the two Gospels has become insipid,

[1] For the Matthean parable cf. Smith, *Parables*, pp. 201 ff.

which suggests a common written source; on the other hand since salt does not really go bad, it is doubtful whether the word is not used in reference to the disciple who has 'turned foolish' in the LXX sense (II Kings xxiv. 10). In this case it would be natural to suppose that the sayings of Luke xiv. 26 f., and 34 f., are drawn by him from a stratum of oral tradition also available to Matthew; as is often the case Luke has preserved the original lack of context, while Matthew has preserved a more original form of the wording. The group of sayings is too short to have circulated in a written form; they may have been appended to the banquet-sayings, but it is hard to see why Matthew has preserved so little.

The saying about carrying the cross is attested by two independent lines of tradition (Mark viii. 34 = Matt. xvi. 24 = Luke ix. 23); it is possible that it owes its preservation to the fact that it was regarded as a prophecy subsequently fulfilled; but the criminal carrying his own cross was a proverbial figure, and the words are a warning that he who would follow Jesus must be prepared to be treated like him as a malefactor.[1] The words thus understood lead admirably up to the sayings which follow about counting the cost of discipleship; unless the hearers are prepared to go to the length of being treated in this way, they cannot be disciples. The crowds that accompany Jesus and lead to the saying are no doubt a Lucan editorial insertion; they are appropriate to the warning to those who 'come' to Jesus.[2] On the other hand they are entirely inappropriate to the supposed scene at dinner in the Pharisee's house. It would seem that Luke has inserted a collection of unattached sayings with a dramatic introduction of his own, forgetting the scene presupposed

---

[1] For the saying cf. Vol. 1, p. 64, n. 1. [For another view see now E. Dinkler in *N.T. Studien f. Bultmann* (1954), pp. 110–29.]

[2] καὶ στραφεὶς εἶπεν is a favourite Lucan method of introducing a saying; it is not found in Mark. It is necessitated by the scene in Luke vii. 44 and xxiii. 28, both of which are peculiar to Luke; in vii. 9 (= Matt. viii. 10), ix. 55, x. 22 (in many MSS.) and 23 and here, it is a piece of stylistic editing which improves the description of the scene but is quite unnecessary. In John i. 38 and xx. 16 it could be due to imitation of the Lucan mannerism, but is necessitated by the circumstances. Curiously enough Luke has rewritten the scene of Mark v. 30 (ἐπιστραφεὶς) = Matt. ix. 22 so that the phrase is not necessary. On the other hand he has introduced the detail that the Lord 'turned' and looked on Peter at xxii. 61 unless he is here following a non-Marcan source (cf. Vol. 1, p. 133). ἐπιστραφεὶς also appears in Mark viii. 33 (= στραφεὶς Matt. xvi. 23), but Luke omits the incident. In both cases the detail is necessitated by the scene: Jesus has to turn to address a particular person.

by the source of the first part of the chapter. It is possible that the warning to count the cost in xiv. 27–32 was already joined to 25–7 in the tradition which Luke is following, but there is no reason to suppose that this must have been the case; the whole passage 25–32 is too short for a single tract, and while it may be only part of a larger collection, the rest of which has been omitted, there is no evidence pointing to this conclusion; the fact that Matthew knows Luke xiv. 25 f. but not 28 ff. suggests, though it does not prove, that Luke is compiling here from unattached tradition.

He is certainly doing so in what follows; the sayings on salt are in Mark (ix. 41–50) part of a collection which proceeds on lines of verbal association (Vol. I, p. 67) and their meaning has been lost. There is no reason to suppose that Matthew and Luke are using Mark here (cf. above, p. 17); they seem to have access to a fuller version, in which perhaps the sayings were already interpreted to mean that the disciples are to be the salt of the earth. It would seem that the saying circulated in a more or less fixed form among the Greek-speaking communities in view of the appearance of the peculiar μωραίνω both in Matthew and Luke.[1]

The closing words of xiv. 35, 'He that hath ears to hear let him hear', may be a Lucan addition to round off this group of sayings before he goes on to his next source. Luke preserves the phrase at viii. 8 (= Mark iv. 9) but omits it at viii. 17 (= Mark iv. 23). Otherwise it appears only here in his Gospel. The author of the Apocalypse uses it as a formal conclusion to the letters to the Seven Churches; R. H. Charles (*I.C.C.*, *Revelation*, I, p. lxxxiv) ascribes his use of it to his knowledge of the Gospel tradition rather than to his Hebraic cast of thought, while Wetstein on Matt. xi. 15 quotes a parallel from Aelian (*N.A.* VIII, 1)[2] which is closer than those given by Strack and Billerbeck (*ad loc.*). Thus it is possible that Luke's omission at viii. 17 is fortuitous, not on account of any dislike of the phrase as having a possible Semitic ring, and that he has added it here; on the other hand, it may well have been a solemn warning on the responsibilities of discipleship attached to the saying on salt in the tradition before it reached Luke.

---

[1] The lexicons give no parallel for this use of the word, but μῶρος is used in the sense of insipid. It seems doubtful whether the verb would have been used until the saying had been taken to apply to the disciples as the salt of the earth.

[2] ὅτῳ σχολὴ μανθάνειν, οὗτος ὑπέχων τὰ ὦτα ἀκουέτω.

CHAPTER XII

FORGIVENESS: I

Luke xv might seem at first sight a well-marked unit, consisting of three parables all dealing with forgiveness. The narrative introduction might be suspected of being Lucan but for the fact that Luke would hardly have written ἦσαν δὲ αὐτῷ ἐγγίʒοντες... ἀκούειν αὐτοῦ when he might just as well have written ἤγγιʒον δὲ πάντες... ἀκούειν αὐτοῦ. It remains probable that here as at v. 30 he has introduced διεγόγγυʒον out of fondness for the LXX. The parables of the lost sheep and the lost coin follow. Of these the former appears in Matt. xviii. 12 ff., but the wording differs as widely as it could if the parable was to remain recognizable at all. This might suggest that Matthew is following a different source, especially as he omits the parable of the lost coin. On the other hand he may well have thought that the parable of the lost sheep and the lost coin lent themselves dangerously to an antinomian interpretation, and consequently put the former at the end of his collection of sayings on scandals, thereby destroying the point; it is not now Christ's care for the outcast that is the point, but the danger of causing Christ's little ones to perish. It is probable that the parable was always accompanied by an introduction of the Lucan type, which made it clear that the Pharisees were the ninety and nine just persons, who need no repentance. I cannot agree with Dodd (*Parables of the Kingdom*, p. 119) that 'the reference to the righteous is open to the objection which arose in regard to Mark ii. 17 (did Jesus really teach that there were righteous persons who needed no repentance?)'. He seems to fail to recognize a note of satire which is quite in keeping with the methods of Jesus and the Old Testament prophets (cf. Vol. I, p. 14). Matthew in transferring the parable of the lost sheep has been compelled to omit that of the lost coin, which could hardly stand for a little one who might be caused to stumble. He has also sacrificed the vivid details of Luke xv. 6 and the good Semitic parallelism of xv. 7.

The two parables of the lost sheep and the lost coin lead up to the parable of the prodigal son. This is the longest of the synoptic parables. Creed suggests that Luke may have filled out the original from a shorter form, but rejects Wellhausen's suggestion that we really have two parables, the motif of 25 ff. not appearing in the earlier part of the parable (cf. Smith, pp. 193 ff.). This assumes a knowledge of the history of the tradition which we do not possess. There seems, however, no evidence to support the view that Luke has expanded the story, beyond the general probability that a parable would tend to be worn down in the telling, with the result that the shorter parables are more likely to be original and the longer ones to have undergone expansion by the evangelists or their sources in the development of the Church. It is possible that some of the shorter parables were originally delivered in a longer form and gradually worn down in oral tradition, while others were preserved in their original wording almost from the beginning. In the parable of the prodigal son there are some traces of possible Lucan additions and amendments, but as is normal with Luke the revision is entirely superficial and incomplete.[1] Thus in xv. 12 τὸ ἐπιβάλλον μέρος is a technical term which Luke may have introduced; he may be responsible for the introduction of the syntactic participle in 13 and the genitive absolute in 14. ἀσώτως is, as Creed notes, good Greek (cf. ἀσωτία in Eph. v. 16, Titus i. 6, I Pet. iv. 4, all books well above the general level of New Testament Greek). In xv. 15 on the other hand we get a very clumsy change of subject from the son in the first clause to the citizen in the second, while in the first clause of 16 we go back to the son with no notice of the change; contrast the use of ὁ δέ to distinguish the speakers in the dialogue of 25 ff.[2] This is quite in the style of rabbinical literature, which passes freely from one subject to another in consecutive sentences, with no particle to show that it is doing so. But it is very bad Greek, in which the abundance of relatives, pronouns and particles makes it easy to mark the change of speaker, which in rabbinical literature is left to the imagination and intelligence of the reader.[3] From 15

[1] For a study of Semitisms in the parable cf. J. Jeremias, 'Zum Gleichnis vom verlorenen Sohn', in *Theol. Zeits.* v (1949), pp. 228–31.

[2] Klostermann in *Handbuch z. N.T., ad loc.* compares vii. 15: but this passage is pure 'translation-Greek', cf. *Hellenistic Elements*, p. 1, and contrast Acts xi. 23, xvi. 14 f. and similar passages in Acts.

[3] Two examples chosen at random will show the difference. In *Hagiga* 4b we have a legend telling how the angel of death sent one of his angels to fetch him Magdala

onwards the narrative is mainly paratactic with a bad use of the superfluous αὐτός (note especially verse 20). In 21 we have 'heaven' used in the sense of God; apart from the Matthean 'kingdom of heaven', this use of the rabbinical periphrasis of heaven for God appears in the New Testament only here and in Mark xi. 30 and 31 with the parallels in both synoptic Gospels.[1] Also relevant may be John iii. 27,[2] where there is probably an allusion to the story preserved in the Marcan passage, the implication being that the Baptist's past success has been given him 'from heaven', while the greater success of Jesus shows that he possesses an authority 'from heaven' greater than that of the Baptist. Equally Semitic is the parallelism in 24; Luke would probably have produced a chiasmus if left to himself.[3]

The latter part of the parable shows similar Greek. We have again a rather awkward change of subject in xv. 28; the repeated use of ὁ δέ is again reminiscent of the rabbinical dialogue, though better than a mere repetition of καὶ εἶπεν. In general it may be said that the parable, though not 'translation-Greek', shows that large proportion of 'primary Semitisms' which we should expect in a Semitic author translating from Aramaic with an imperfect knowledge of

the women's hairdresser. 'He went and brought Magdala the infants' teacher. He said to him, I told you to bring the women's hairdresser. He said to him, I will take her back. He said to him, As you have brought her, let her stay.' Here the repeated 'He said to him' performs the part of inverted commas in a modern book; the effect is often extremely puzzling, at any rate to the inexpert. For an example of the same method in narrative cf. *ibid.* 5 b. 'R. Joshua b. Hanina stood before Caesar. A *min* signalled to him with his hand, "A people from whom God has turned away his face". He signalled to him, "His hand is still over us".' This appears to be recognized as perfectly good writing in rabbinical literature, but it would be very bad Greek, as is the change of subject in three clauses only introduced by 'and' in Luke xv. 16 and 17 a.

[1] For the rabbinical use cf. Str.-B. on Matt. xxi. 25.

[2] In view of John iii. 31 it is doubtful whether John iii. 27 should be interpreted as meaning 'from God' or 'from heaven' as the source from which the power of God comes; cf. Jas. i. 17.

[3] The ring in xv. 22 is peculiar; Str.-B. and Wetstein *ad loc.* produce no real parallels. Klostermann suggests a reminiscence of Gen. xli. 42, but if so the reminiscence is a very confused one; the ring is given as a sign that Joseph is to be viceroy, not when he is being washed and reclothed on being taken out of prison (Gen. xli. 14). I can find no evidence of a custom of giving a ring to an honoured guest as opposed to a trusted agent for whom it is a sign of delegated authority; for the latter use cf. Esther iii. 10 and viii. 2; I Macc. vi. 15.

Greek (cf. de Zwaan in *The Beginnings of Christianity*, II, 53 f.); they survive in Luke because he has never seriously tried to adapt his source to the Greek style of which he is capable at his best, in part perhaps because he regards this type of Greek as the style of 'sacred prose' (de Zwaan, *loc. cit.*).

So far we might have had a single document of three parables. Suspicion is, however, aroused by the extreme difference in length between the first two and that of the prodigal son. We should not naturally expect so long a parable to be derived from the same line of tradition as two of the more normal length as represented by the parables of the lost coin and the lost sheep. Moreover, the opening of Luke xvi is peculiarly abrupt for the opening of a new tract; it would be natural in a series of sayings or parables to find the later sayings introduced with a bare formula, but not the first. It must in any case be recognized that we have some such transition somewhere; the parable of the prodigal son has the absolute minimum of 'and he said', while the story of Dives and Lazarus as it stands has no opening at all, though, as will be seen, this is misleading. On the other hand it would be easier for Luke to omit an introduction before the parable of the prodigal son than before the parable of the unjust steward. For the parable of the prodigal son simply carries on the thought of the preceding parables; if it ever had narrative opening, as it probably had, that opening may well have been little more than a doublet of the opening of the parables of the lost sheep and the lost coin. It would be reasonable to eliminate a second narrative introduction at 11 and replace it by the bare 'and he said'. It would not be reasonable to suppress an opening to the parable of the unjust steward. It will be seen below that there are good grounds for supposing that this is actually the case, and that the parables of xv. 3–10 originally ended with the sayings of xvii. 1–10 or at least some of them.

CHAPTER XIII

GOD AND MAMMON

The parables of Luke xvi clearly do not deal with the theme of God's joy in welcoming back the repentant sinner, and have no obvious claim to belong to the same source as the preceding group of parables. On the other hand it is perfectly possible that with the parable of the prodigal son they formed a compilation of longer parables, the principle of combination in this case being simply the formal one that they were all told at length in a narrative form.

The parable of the unjust steward as it stands is quite inexplicable; it seems impossible to find a reasonable explanation except on the hypothesis of a primitive corruption of the text. At the risk of adding yet another hypothesis to the innumerable forlorn attempts to explain its meaning I would suggest that the explanation lies in a fairly simple piece of haplography. The parable in its original form was a counterpart of the parable of the merciless debtor (Matt. xviii. 23), but described how the steward forgave his lord's debtors, and as a result was not merely commended by his master but actually restored. It was followed by several independent sayings introduced with the formula 'And the Lord said'. Thus the original text of xvi. 8 ran:[1]

KAIEΠHNECENOKC̄TONOIKONOMON
THCAΔIKIACOTIΦPONIMωCEΠOIHCEN
KAIAΠEKATECTHCENEICTHNOIKONOMIAN
KAIEIΠENOKC̄OTIOIYIOITOYAIωNOC ...

Here the three opening καί with π in close proximity led to the omission of the clause καὶ ἀπεκατέστησεν αὐτὸν εἰς τὴν οἰκονομίαν which thus reached Luke in a form in which the point was already lost; the omission of 'and the Lord said' before 'that the children of this world . . .' is due to Luke who supposed that the 'lord' who

---

[1] For the use of contractions for *nomina sacra* at an early date in Christian (or possibly pre-Christian Jewish) literature, cf. Bell and Skeat, *Fragments of an Unknown Gospel*, pp. 2–4.

I am indebted to Professor Sir E. H. Minns for helping me in regard to the palaeographic possibilities of such an error. Naturally he is not responsible for my conclusions.

praised the steward at the beginning of 8 was Jesus, whereas it was really the rich man of the parable.[1] In Luke's source the sayings of xvi. 8–12 had already been added to the parable; if authentic, they had no original connexion with the parable but were added simply as a result of verbal association (Mammon), unless indeed they were collected and added here in order to counteract any possible misunderstanding that might be caused by a too literal acceptance of the parable at its face value. We have a similar expansion of a parable by other words of Jesus at Luke xviii. 6 ff. where, as will be seen below (pp. 110 ff.), there is reason to believe that the verses represent an addition to the parable of sayings which had no real connexion with it, possibly in circles connected with St Paul,[2] the parable being again one which *prima facie* involves an ethical difficulty. In xviii. 6 ff. the addition seems an attempt to introduce a saying which had no fixed home in the tradition by a not very skilful explanation of the parable of the unjust judge; here the motive may have been to point out that Jesus did not really encourage financial dishonesty in his followers by adding sayings which taught the precise opposite of the *prima facie* meaning of the parable.

On this hypothesis the saying that the children of this world are in their generation wiser than the children of light was originally unattached. It may simply have been a criticism of the folly of some pious people on some particular occasion, comparable to Matt. x. 16b ('be wise as serpents') which Luke seems to have found too shocking to include in his Gospel; or it may have been intended to teach the lesson of the parable by contrasting the folly of the righteous who refuse to pardon those who injure them with the worldly wisdom of the steward. Luke xvi. 9, a separate saying,

---

[1] It has been suggested (cf. Creed *ad loc.*) that 'the lord' here really refers to Jesus. But there is no parallel in the synoptic gospels for a quotation of the words of Jesus in *oratio obliqua*.

[2] If we suppose that the phrase καὶ εἶπεν ὁ κύριος has dropped out we should have a close similarity in view of the Hebraic use of the genitive τῆς ἀδικίας in both cases. Naturally the fact that the word is the same in each case cannot be pressed; but the qualifying genitive in both cases is suggestive. And it may be noted that Luke vi. 8 and 9 and xviii. 6 and the Pauline Epistles (not counting II Tim. ii. 19) account for fifteen out of twenty-six uses of the word ἀδικία in the New Testament. It is not found in the synoptics except in these passages and Luke xiii. 27 where it represents the ἀνομία of Ps. vi. 9 and Matt. vii. 23. But this may be pure chance: ἀδικία is frequent in the LXX.

seems to mean 'Make worldly wealth your friend, in order that when it fails you, as it must when you die, they (i.e. God) may receive you in heaven', an ironical comment on the folly of seeking riches.[1] The remaining verses clearly teach the precise opposite of the *prima facie* moral of the parable of the unjust steward: if you are not faithful in worldly things you cannot expect to be entrusted with heavenly treasure. Luke has transferred 13 from its original place in the Sermon on the Plain in order to make it abundantly clear that the parable was not to be taken as a guide to Christian conduct (cf. above, pp. 29, 69). It seems likely that the other sayings were at any rate originally unattached to any particular point in the tradition; whether they were added by Luke or a previous compiler cannot be said, though the obscurity of verse 12 suggests that it came to him in its present form and that he incorporated it as it stood without asking what it meant.[2]

It might be objected to the explanation of the parable of the unjust steward suggested above that whereas the steward forgives sins against his master the Christian has no power to forgive sins against God but only sins against himself.[3] But the parable need only be concerned with its central point (cf. Smith, p. 18); the unedifying character of the steward does not impair the lesson 'Forgive, if you seek to be forgiven' any more than the unedifying character of the unjust judge impairs the lesson 'persevere in prayer'. The above explanation can, of course, be put forward only as a conjecture; but the omission of a line as a result of haplography is easy and the resulting confusion, added to the unedifying character

---

[1] Creed, following Wellhausen, interprets it to mean that the disciples are to use wealth so as to make it their friend, in order that when they die God may receive them into heaven. But in the ethics of Jesus the only right use of wealth is to get rid of it.

[2] I make the assumption that ἡμέτερον is the correct reading. 'Ours' followed by 'you' is clumsy; it is still harder to suppose that 'Jesus sets himself along with other heirs in the kingdom' (Creed). If this reading is right, I should be inclined to guess that the saying comes from the early Church and was intended to warn off would-be converts who hoped to escape from the consequences of their misdeeds by becoming Christians (cf. Lucian, *Peregrinus*, 11). But ἡμέτερον is very difficult and may be merely due to a slip of the pen, though it has the prescriptive right of the harder reading.

[3] But the objection is not entirely valid if the steward is responsible for paying a lump sum to his master and collecting the dues from the tenants who are 'debtors' for a certain fixed amount. By encouraging them to falsify the return of what they owe, he forgives them what is due to himself since he will have a larger deficit to make up. For the type of procedure cf. Grier, *Accounting in the Zenon Papyri*, p. 50.

of the steward, explains the chaotic amplification of the parable in the verses which follow.[1]

The rest of this source continued with the conventional interruption; here it is the Pharisees who interrupt on the ground of their covetousness. The interruption is needed to introduce the third long parable, that of Dives and Lazarus (xvi. 19–31); whether the interrupters in the source were represented as Pharisees or not cannot be said. In reality the Pharisees would not have seen anything that they did not believe themselves in the doctrine that one cannot serve God and Mammon; the bad Pharisee, as described in Talmudic sources (cf. Str.-B. IV, 336 f.), would be enough of a hypocrite to pretend to accept the teaching of Luke xvi. 10 ff., even though he was in the habit of 'devouring widows' houses'. The appearance of the literary word φιλάργυρος (in New Testament only here and II Tim. iii. 2)[2] and the LXX word ἐκμυκτηρίζω (in New Testament only here and Luke xxiii. 35; four times in LXX)[3] suggests that Luke may well have rewritten his source; it may have contained a different interruption by a Pharisee, or it may have described how Jesus' teaching was ridiculed by some who were not Pharisees. If Luke has preserved the sense of his source correctly, it comes from a milieu which already regarded the Pharisees as the villains of the piece. But this view of them might have developed any time after the Crucifixion, especially among Jewish converts who had always shared the popular opposition to the Pharisees.

At Luke xvi. 16 there is a quite intolerable break in the arrangement. Verses 16–18 consist of three detached sayings which have no claim to their present context and no connexion with anything that precedes or follows them. They are followed by the parable of Dives and Lazarus, which appears with no introductory formula. It has no relation to the Christian law of divorce (xvi. 18). On the other hand it is exactly appropriate to the theme of 15 as showing how Dives, though exalted in the sight of men, was abominable in

---

[1] The omission would be all the easier if, as is suggested in this book, Luke's source is not a single book but a series of catechetical tracts copied out as needed for itinerant teachers of local catechists. We have to allow for a large amount of copying out at a low literary level.

[2] The noun also in I Tim. vi. 10.

[3] The compounded verb is stated in Moulton and Milligan, *Voc.Gr.N.T.* s.v., to be rare outside the LXX.

the sight of God. Now a parable can be introduced without an introductory 'and he said', 'he spake also another parable' or some similar phrase, where it is simply an amplification of the preceding saying. Thus in Matt. xxi. 28 ff. the parable of the two sons is attached to the question as to the Baptist's authority by the question 'What think ye?' But, as it stands, it serves to amplify the preceding utterance and so no fresh introduction is needed. (It is of course immaterial here whether the original parable dealt with the Baptist; Matt. xxi. 31 and 33 look like a not very successful attempt to attach the parable to the controversy concerning him.) At Matt. xxi. 33 we have another parable with no narrative introduction; but this is replaced by the words 'hear another parable'. We have also a short collection of parables in Matt. xiii. 44–50, again without a narrative introduction, and the opening at 44 is very abrupt; the abruptness, however, is due to the fact that the interpretation of the parable of the tares has been inserted by Matthew. It would seem that originally there were two collections each containing a triad of parables, the first triad having narrative introductions, the latter not. These were combined together with Matt. xxi. 51 f. as a conclusion. The change from parables with a narrative introduction to those without one would be very abrupt, but the collections serve the needs of men who had neither knowledge nor care for literary style; the abruptness is made worse by Matthew's insertion of the interpretation of the parable of the tares. In any case all the parables in the collection deal with the same theme, the kingdom of heaven, and have a suitable opening formula, 'the kingdom of heaven is like . . .'.

In Luke xvi, however, we have no continuity whatsoever, in view of verses 16–18. Without them we get an excellent connexion of subject. The lack of a narrative introduction appears to be without a parallel in Luke; but he is often content with a bare minimum of introduction; thus at xv. 11 we simply have 'And he said' as an introduction to the parable of the prodigal son. Here he may have felt that the parable ran on so naturally from the answer to the Pharisees that no introduction was necessary. More probably the parable simply stood without introduction in his source, and he did not trouble to change it.

On the other hand verses 16–18 cannot simply be omitted; there is no manuscript evidence that at any stage they did not form part of the text of Luke's Gospel.[1] The only possible explanation would seem to be that these unattached sayings came into the possession of a previous owner of the copy of the tract or of Luke himself and that they were jotted down in the margin; thence they were inadvertently allowed to creep into the text. It would be easiest for this to happen at the top and bottom of the page of a manuscript in the form of a codex; in this case it would seem that they were inserted in this way by Luke himself; it is also possible that they were jotted down by the owner of the first copy of the Gospel or the copy from which all our existing texts are derived.[2] The omission of 16–18 gives a clear connexion of meaning, which is precisely that of the Egyptian folk-tale from which the story is derived; it is not, as in the Jewish versions, adapted to Jewish views by the explanation that the poor man was righteous and the rich man wicked (cf. Creed, *ad loc.*). It is no doubt to be presumed that this point was made clearer in the original; Luke had no need to insist on it, since the story was uttered as a rebuke to the Pharisees, and the rich man is to be regarded as a specimen of that conventional villain, the covetous Pharisee.

[1] They stood in Marcion's text (Tert. *adv. Marc.* IV, 33–4). It is curious that he did not delete them in view of their approval of Moses and the prophets. Cf. Harnack, *Marcion*², pp. 55 and 220*.

[2] For a similar confusion caused by the fact that a marginal note has found its way into the text cf. Diod. Sic. XII, 40 and Jacoby's note on Ephorus, from whom the passage is drawn, in *F.G.H.* 70, F. 196. According to Diodorus, Aristophanes described Pericles in the lines of *Pax* 603 ff., ending ὥστε τῷ καπνῷ πάντας Ἕλληνας δακρῦσαι, τούς τ' ἐκεῖ τούς τ' ἐνθάδε (*Pax* 611). καὶ πάλιν ἐν ἄλλοις Εὔπολις ὁ ποιητής· Περικλέης οὐλύμπιος ἤστραπτεν, ἐβρόντα, συνεκύκα τὴν Ἑλλάδα. πειθώ τις ἐπεκάθιζεν ἐπὶ τοῖς χείλεσιν. οὕτως ἐκήλει, καὶ μόνος τῶν ῥητόρων τὸ κέντρον ἐγκατέλειπε τοῖς ἀκροωμένοις. But Περικλέης ... χείλεσιν comes not from Eupolis but from Aristophanes (*Ach.* 530). It appears from Aristodemus, who also reproduces the same passage of Ephorus, that the original passage contained the two quotations from Aristophanes (*F.G.H.* 104, F. 16). It would seem that Diodorus or an early copyist inserted in the margin the quite different view of Eupolis (Kock, *Fr. Com. Gr.* I, 281, 94), and that this has found its way into the text with the result that Eupolis is credited with two lines of Aristophanes. Jacoby holds that the insertion may go back to Diodorus himself. For a similar interpolation cf. *F.G.H.* 183, T. 1 where it is said that Caecilius of Caleacte practised as a sophist in Rome ἐπὶ τοῦ Σεβαστοῦ Καίσαρος καὶ ἕως Ἀδριανοῦ καὶ ἀπὸ δούλων ὥς τινες ἱστορήκασι (Suidas, s.v. Καικίλιος). This is obviously absurd; presumably this Caecilius has been confused with another who lived till the principate of Hadrian. It would seem that the original text of Suidas ran Καίσαρος· ἦν δὲ καὶ ἀπὸ δούλων ὥς τινες ἱστορήκασι. Someone who confused him with the other Caecilius added καὶ ἕως Ἀδριανοῦ in a marginal note which has again found its way into the text.

The sayings inserted in Luke xvi. 16–18 seem to have been unattached traditional sayings. Matthew has found a home for Luke xvi. 16 at Matt. xi. 12 f., a position clearly due to himself; it cannot be supposed that Luke would have transferred it from so good a position to its present place where it is completely irrelevant to the context. On the other hand the Matthean form is probably nearer the original; it would seem to have meant that from the days of the Baptist the kingdom of heaven suffers violence at the hands of the Zealot movement and that the zealots 'plunder' it by seeking to exploit it by violence for their own advantage. Luke, however, appears to have lost all clue to the meaning (as Matthew probably had too) and took βιάζεται as the middle in the sense of 'forcing its way in'.[1] For the thought of the kingdom of God forcing its way in he substituted the conventional εὐαγγελίζεται, while he used his interpretation of βιάζομαι to describe mankind in general, notably no doubt the Gentiles, as forcing their way into the kingdom of God. It is of course possible that the saying had been modified before it reached Luke; in any case we have here a short epigrammatic saying preserved in the tradition after its meaning had been lost. xvi. 17 is a similar unattached saying; it is noteworthy that Luke has preserved it in spite of its apparent insistence on the permanence of the Torah. There is no evidence that he derived it from the same written source as Matthew since the two sayings could hardly differ more widely in their wording. The Matthean position of the saying in the Sermon on the Mount is clearly due to Matthew. The new law of divorce is again a saying which would naturally circulate in an almost fixed form in the community; the four forms in which the saying appears (Matt. v. 31, xix. 9, Mark x. 11 f. and the Lucan version) seem to come from a common oral tradition which is preserved most closely in the two last passages. It is possible that Luke considered this particular verse so important that he jotted it down as a point to be preserved out of Mark, while the incident to which Mark attached it seemed too Jewish to be worth recording. There is no reason to suppose that these fragments reached Luke and Matthew in a common written form.

[1] For this sense cf. Polybius II, 38, 7 (where it has an active force) and Plutarch, *Timoleon*, IX, 240 A.

CHAPTER XIV

FORGIVENESS: II

The section of Luke (xvii. 1–6) following the story of Dives and Lazarus, with its Matthean parallels, throws a considerable light on the methods of the two evangelists. It has been noted above (p. 92) that there are reasons for suspecting that in Luke's source the parables of the lost sheep and the lost coin did not really lead on to that of the prodigal son, and that the last came to Luke as one of a set of three long narrative parables. If we take out these three as a separate source, incorporated bodily by Luke into another collection of sayings which opened with the first two, we find that:

> Luke xv. 3–6 = Matt. xviii. 12–14
> Luke xvii. 1 b = Matt. xviii. 6 f.
> Luke xvii. 3 = Matt. xviii. 15
> Luke xvii. 4 = Matt. xviii. 21 f.
> Luke xvii. 6 = Matt. xvii. 20.

There was an obvious reason for Luke's insertion of his three long parables after those of the lost sheep and the lost coin, namely that the latter served as an admirable introduction to the parable of the prodigal son; he could hardly be expected to take the trouble to break up his second collection and transfer the parables of the unjust steward and of Dives and Lazarus to a more suitable context; he simply inserted the three long parables in a single block and returned to the collection, which opened with the two short parables, and went on from the sayings on God's care for the lost to the duty of avoiding scandals, which might lead to their loss, and ended with some miscellaneous sayings.

Matthew on the other hand saw that the saying on faith (Luke xvii. 5 f.) had no logical connexion with its context, and that it could stand very well as the conclusion of the healing of the demoniac boy; he transferred it to xvii. 20. He proceeded to the sections of Mark which follow the demoniac boy (Matt. xvii. 22 f.= Mark ix. 30–2, and Matt. xviii. 1–4 = Mark ix. 33–7 revised by conflation with the other Marcan story of Jesus calling a little child in Mark x. 13 ff., and by the omission of the unedifying wrangle of the Twelve for precedence). Naturally he omitted the story of the strange exorcist (Mark ix. 38–40); it might easily have been used as a justification of the Pauline missions, of which Matthew never approves though he cannot entirely condemn them (cf. above, p. 19). The Marcan saying on a cup of cold water (Mark ix. 41) he had already used at x. 42. Meanwhile, he inserts at xvii. 24 ff. the story of the coin in the fish's mouth; it had to come here since in the Marcan story it was the last occasion when Jesus was in Capernaum, and therefore the last point in the narrative at which Peter could conveniently be sent out to catch a fish.[1]

This brings Matthew at xviii. 6 to the Marcan sayings on scandals (Mark ix. 42 ff.). Into them he inserts from the non-Marcan source which he shares with Luke the woe on those who are responsible for causing scandals, however inevitable the coming of scandals may be; it is probable that this source contained an independent version of the saying on the mill-stone since it appears here in Luke, though he is not here following Mark; it is of course possible that the wording of Luke xvii. 2 has been affected by his memories of the Marcan version.[2] Matthew preserves the Marcan sayings on cutting off the hand or foot in an abbreviated form; there is no evidence that there was any source for these except Mark ix. 43 ff., as Matthew follows Mark closely and introduces no new elements; Luke would in any case have omitted them out of regard for the Greek dislike of mutilation. He has also omitted them after ix. 50, where he follows Mark ix. 33 ff. as far as 40, but then omits the sayings about scandals, since he had them elsewhere, and entirely omits the cutting off of hand or foot, going on to the beginning of the journey to Jerusalem. On the other hand he has at xvii. 7–10 the saying on unprofitable servants, which has some suspiciously

---

[1] For the construction and origins of the story in the conditions of Jewish Christianity in the period A.D. 70–96, cf. Kilpatrick, *Origins*, p. 42. It would be interesting to speculate whether the rabbinical parallels (cf. Str.-B. on Matt. xvii. 27) and this verse reflect a knowledge of the story of Polycrates (Herodotus, III, 41 and Strabo, XIV, 1, 16 apparently from a different source), transformed into the theme of a folk-tale, or whether Polycrates is an independent specimen of the same motif.

[2] The difference between Luke xvii. 1 b and Matt. xviii. 7 represents independent editing of a saying: ἀνάγκη ἐλθεῖν τὰ σκάνδαλα, οὐαὶ δὲ δι' οὖ ἔρχεται.

good syntax and a very good ending with two cretics. Luke has certainly done some rewriting here. But it is normal for these tracts to have a striking ending, and xvii. 6 would be a very weak one. On the other hand 10 would make a good one. No doubt in the double cretic we discern the hand of Luke himself, either as a deliberate use of rhetorical methods or as a result of his natural sense of Greek; but without it the saying about unprofitable servants is a very effective ending. Moreover, its omission by Matthew might well be due to its conflict with the formal Jewish view of the reward for the observance of the Torah (cf. Moore, *Judaism*, II, pp. 92 ff., where, however, Moore minimizes, as he often does, the very real difference between such passages as this and the normal rabbinical outlook).

It is, however, possible that the collection only went as far as xvii. 4. Up to this point we have a good connexion of thought. The main theme is forgiveness; the first two parables deal with God's forgiveness of the sinner. This, however, might lead to a real problem, since it could be interpreted as a license to do evil that good may come. The problem was particularly urgent in the Pauline communities, since Paul had repudiated the whole conception of law as binding on the Christian; any admission of the idea of law would allow his Jewish opponents to reply that the element of law which the Christian still needed was provided by the law of Moses. But even in Jewish-Christian circles the teaching of the parables of the lost sheep and the lost coin might be taken to encourage the sinner to postpone repentance. Hence the sayings on not causing scandals would naturally be appended to the parables of forgiveness; God's forgiveness carries with it the duty of not causing one's brother to stumble. The implied moral is that of Rom. xiv. 13 ff. and I Cor. viii. 9 ff.

Thus it is possible that the tract ended with the sayings on forgiveness of one's brother, and that the sayings of Luke xvii. 5–10 owe their position to Luke, who found them isolated in the tradition that came to him; the appearance of the grain of mustard seed at Matt. xvii. 20 and Luke xvii. 6 is simply due to coincidence. But on the whole, since a collection of sayings consisting merely of Luke xv. 1–10 and xvii. 1–4 would be rather short, it is more likely that the sayings on the grain of mustard seed and probably also on the unprofitable servants were included in the original collection of sayings in spite of their irrelevance; it is in favour of this that the request of 'the apostles' in xvii. 5 comes where we should expect an interruption.

The sayings of Luke xvii. 3 ff. are of interest as showing Matthew's methods of dealing with the material at his disposal. After the parable of the lost sheep he has introduced a fragment of a 'Church order' (for which see below, pp. 133 f.). From this he goes back to the source which he shares with Luke; but he had a variation of the saying of Luke xvii. 4 which may already have been introduced in his version by the conventional question from Peter (cf. Creed on Luke x. 1). The whole section in Matthew concludes with the parable of the unmerciful servant (for which cf. below, p. 134). This rearrangement secures a good logical sequence, which has no claim to be original.

Luke's version of the saying on the grain of mustard seed seems close to the original form of the saying. The saying itself circulated in two traditions, since we also find it in Mark xi. 22 f. (= Matt. xxi. 21). In this version the element of faith has been exaggerated in a purely mechanical fashion: the faith needed has become complete freedom from doubt that the prayer has already been 'as good as answered' in its literal sense.[1] This conception of faith as a mechanical means of working miracles can of course be paralleled in rabbinical writings; and faith is one of the means by which such miracles are guaranteed; but on the whole rabbinical theology condemns this conception of prayer as a magical means of eliciting miracles.[2] With the Marcan text we may compare Jas. i. 6 where there is a blend of the Marcan view that the man who prays with a doubtful mind will not get what he wants and the philosophical commonplace which condemns the 'double-minded' or 'half-hearted' man (cf. Philo, *De Post. Cain.* 100). In both passages we find διακρίνομαι used in the sense of 'doubt', a sense which, except

---

[1] Both Rawlinson and Klostermann *ad loc.* try to avoid the conclusion that the text, as it stands, promises an automatic fulfilment of any prayer, provided that the petitioner has absolute faith that 'he has received' already what he asks for. This seems merely an attempt to manipulate the text in the interest of orthodoxy. Whether the Marcan text is original is another matter.

[2] Cf. Moore, *Judaism*, pp. 206 and 232 ff., and the examples in Montefiore and Loewe, *A Rabbinical Anthology*, pp. 344 ff.

for this passage in Mark and its Matthean parallel, is confined to the more Hellenistic books of the New Testament (Acts x. 20; Rom. iv. 20; Jas. i. 6 and ii. 4[1]). The appearance of the word in James and Mark in a precisely similar context in which doubt is an automatic hindrance to an answer to prayer, which otherwise is sure to be answered, suggests that the Marcan version of the saying may have passed through circles akin to those from which the Epistle of James is derived.

The suspicion that the Marcan version is secondary and the Lucan nearer to the original is increased by the fact that from purely Jewish circles the removing of a tree by faith is more natural than the removing of a mountain by faith, since the 'remover of mountains' is in rabbinical literature not the man who can work miracles but the man whose knowledge of the Torah and the methods of interpreting it can 'remove mountains' in the way of setting aside apparent difficulties (cf. Str.-B. on Matt. xvii. 20). On the other hand the removal of a tree by its roots was a miracle performed by R. Eliezer (c. 90) in order to prove his point (cf. Str.-B. *loc. cit.*). Further it may be noted that Luke's 'this sycamine-tree' has an air of vividness which suggests that it may be original; Mark has 'this mountain' at xi. 23, but it does not appear what 'this mountain' is, since we have not heard anything of a mountain in the context. On the other hand the fact that the Marcan version of the saying is attached to the story of the barren tree suggests that possibly the first compiler who attached the saying to this miracle had the story before him in a form which referred to a συκάμινος or a συκῆ, and attached it by a process of verbal assimilation; the change of the fig tree into a mountain may then reflect a purely Christian practice of using 'faith which can remove mountains' as a proverb. Thus it is at least

---

[1] The first passage is from the Hellenistic running commentary on a set of Jewish maxims which forms Jas. i and iii; the second from one of the diatribes, but here meaning rather 'to be divided in your attitude', i.e. to be inconsistent, than 'to be divided in your mind', i.e. to doubt. The word here seems to be on its way to the meaning 'doubt', whereas in Jas. i. 6 as in Mark it has arrived. (For the structure of James cf. my article in *J.T.S.* XLVI (1945), 10 ff.) Sanday and Headlam on Rom. iv. 20 hold that the usage originates in the New Testament 'or in near proximity to Christianity'. Büchsel (in *T.W.z.N.T.* III, 950) derives it from the use of the Aramaic פלג in this sense, but this is hardly confirmed by its predominance in Hellenistic writers of the New Testament.

probable that Luke here preserves the saying in its original form and that his source represents an older line of tradition than the Marcan.[1]

[1] Creed *ad loc.* regards it as probable that the introduction of the συκάμινος 'far less congruous as a metaphor than the mountain' is due to Luke's recollection of the Marcan fig tree. But this ignores the fact that in rabbinical literature 'removing mountains' has a quite different meaning. Wetstein's parallels for 'removing mountains' in the sense of 'performing impossibilities' are drawn from Greek and Latin literature; he quotes Job ix. 5 and xxviii. 9, but here we are dealing with removing mountains as manifestations of divine omnipotence; R. Samuel in *Baba Bathra* 3 b speaks of the imperial government as saying 'I remove mountains' and refusing to withdraw, but here the point is the folly of resisting its decrees.

CHAPTER XV

THE NON-MARCAN APOCALYPSE

After the parable of the grain of mustard seed Luke follows his normal practice of using a gap between his sources for introducing unattached fragments, in this case the servant's reward (xvii. 7–10) and the story of the ten lepers (xvii. 11–19). The latter story appears to have been drawn from a source interested in the relation of Jesus to the Samaritans (cf. Dibelius, *Formgesch. d. Evang.*, p. 120). As it stands it is used to enhance the impression of Jesus' journey to Jerusalem; it is clearly out of place in a journey which is to end at Jericho. Linguistically the passage is curious; it contains one of the two cases in the synoptists in which the word εὐχαριστεῖν is used in the sense of 'giving thanks' in the ordinary, as against the liturgical or quasi-liturgical sense.[1] On the other hand in verses 11 and 14 the use of ἐγένετο followed by a main verb, in one case with καί, in the other without, is not Luke's own usage when he is not following a source or anxious to produce a hieratic effect, which is certainly not the case in 14 (cf. Creed on Luke i. 8), while the αὐτοί of 13 is entirely unnecessary and very clumsy. All we can say of the story is that it appears to have come from a Palestinian source and to have taken on a slight Hellenistic colouring on its way to Luke;[2] the source in question may, of course, have been the early Christian community of Samaria.

The incident is followed by a short apocalypse (xvii. 20–37) which would seem to have formed an independent unit. It is opened with an introductory question; after this it goes on with 'And he said to his disciples'. The apocalypse itself forms a single whole and there is no need therefore for any further use of a formula such as 'and he said'; but at the end we have the conventional question

---

[1] For the miracles of feeding cf. my *Hellenistic Elements*, p. 9.

[2] In view of this Hellenistic tinge, and the almost Pauline ring of the servant's reward (xvii. 7–10), it is possible that these pieces were attached to the tract from which Luke took the unjust judge, the Pharisee and the publican, and perhaps also the pounds (see below), in which case the insertion of the apocalypse, which dislocates the source, was presumably suggested by the language of the unjust judge. Some place had to be found for it.

and answer. The fact that the sources of which the Gospels are compilations normally begin with a narrative introduction in which a question is addressed to Jesus makes it probable that xvii. 20 f. stood in Luke's source; we cannot check the point from Matthew since he has simply broken up this apocalypse into fragments and inserted the fragments into his version of the Marcan apocalypse.[1]

On the other hand there is no reason for supposing that the question of the Pharisees and Jesus' answer are in their original position. There is no suggestion that the question is asked in a hostile sense, either in the question itself or in the answer of Jesus. Moreover, the answer appears to be totally inconsistent with the apocalypse which follows. However we translate 'among you' (i.e. already present) or 'within you' (i.e. an inward reality in the hearts of its members), the answer appears to be a refusal to enter into apocalyptic speculations of the kind which immediately follows.[2] The saying would appear to have survived independently and only to have been joined to the apocalypse by a compiler who wanted a suitable narrative with a question and answer to introduce his apocalypse, and considered that any question and answer that had anything to do with the kingdom of God was good enough to serve his purpose.[3] Thus there is no reason to suppose that it does not

[1] Luke xvii. 33 has been omitted as having already appeared in Matthew's eschatological amplification of the charge to the Twelve (x. 39) and in its Marcan position (Matt. xvi. 25=Mark viii. 35). The saying with minor verbal differences would seem to have had a wide currency, and there is no need to suppose that Matthew deliberately transferred it from this apocalypse to the charge to the Twelve; it is more probable that he inserted the saying there as a widely known and appropriate text, and omitted it here as having already been used on two occasions. Otherwise all the matter of this apocalypse which he needed has simply been inserted into the structure of Mark xiii.

[2] Cf. Vol. I, p. 112. Creed suggests as a further possible interpretation 'the kingdom, when it comes, will be suddenly in your midst', treating ἔρχεται as a prophetic present, the sense being that of verse 24; the kingdom of heaven will not appear in a particular corner of the world but everywhere simultaneously. But this is a very difficult sense, and not an answer to the question of the Pharisees.

[3] Bultmann, p. 24, comments on the fact that the saying, though of Palestinian origin, is put into a typical Greek form corresponding to that used for the apophthegms of Greek philosophers. But this only means that Luke on this occasion took the trouble to alter an original ἐπηρώτησαν δὲ αὐτὸν οἱ Φαρισαῖοι ... καὶ ἀπεκρίθη αὐτοῖς καὶ εἶπεν into its present form. Why he should have done so here and not, for example, at xviii. 18 where he has inserted the quite gratuitous detail that the questioner of Mark x. 17 was a 'ruler', it is quite impossible to say. But there is no evidence that Luke has been responsible for more than a trifling alteration of style.

date from the period when Jesus was on quite friendly terms with the Pharisees and that it does not record a genuine incident, though one that had no connexion with the apocalypse.[1] When this is recognized it would seem that Creed's objection to the translation of ἐντὸς ὑμῶν as 'within you', i.e. as a spiritual condition, on the ground that such a saying is inappropriate as addressed to the Pharisees, disappears; we have to recognize once again a saying which survived although it implied a situation which had really become unintelligible in the light of the later development of the quarrel between the Church and the religious leaders of Judaism as a result of the Crucifixion. Creed's further objection that the kingdom of God is nowhere else used to express an inward state of the soul is very doubtful; to sell all for the kingdom of heaven because it is a pearl of great price or in order to buy it because it is a field with a hidden treasure comes near to describing it as an inward spiritual state; there is no need to understand this in the Hellenized sense of P. Oxy. 654 (see below, p. 152). It is more important that the parallel usage in Rom. xiv. 17 is likely to be derived from this text and similar passages where the kingdom is a force at work on earth of an undefined character rather than vice versa, as Creed suggests.[2]

[1] Bultmann, p. 55, objects that the Pharisees had no specific interest in the eschatological question. This seems entirely unjustified by the evidence. Some Pharisees were no doubt more interested in eschatology than others and some, like Jesus himself, may have discouraged speculation; but it may be doubted whether any were without interest. No doubt the phrase 'the Pharisees' here as elsewhere is coloured by the later usage of the Church; it is of course possible that the original questioners were not Pharisees at all, but there is no reason to suppose that 'certain who were Pharisees' would not be completely accurate as an account of the incident.

[2] The usage is unique in Pauline writings. In Paul the kingdom is either an eschatological force at work on earth (I Cor. iv. 20, Col. i. 13, iv. 11), heaven as a state to be attained by the righteous, presumably after its establishment at the Second Coming (I Cor. vi. 9 and 10, xiv. 40, Gal. v. 21 (Eph. v. 5), I Thess. ii. 12, II Thess. i. 5), or the Messianic kingdom between the Second Coming and the end (a curious attempt to syncretize Jewish-Christian apocalyptic with popular Stoicism, cf. *Gentiles*, p. 128). In Acts it is always the first of these senses, except in i. 6 where the 'kingdom' is the temporary Messianic kingdom on earth which the disciples wrongly expect in the near future. The term was not popular in the Hellenistic Church (it is used eight times in Acts, twelve times in the Pauline Epistles including Ephesians), probably for reasons which I have suggested elsewhere (*Jerusalem*, p. 271, nn. 7 and 8). It was too deeply embedded in the Gospels and presumably in popular Jewish-Christian homiletic to be eliminated entirely; but it seems unlikely that Paul would have invented a new use of it, and more likely that he slipped into current

The apocalypse itself is chiefly noticeable for some Lucan adaptations to the current ideas by means of which Judaism in the Dispersion tried to prove that Moses had actually described the periodical devastations of the world by fire and water which Plato had guessed at in the *Timaeus*, and for some typically fine Lucan writing.[1] Lot's wife in xvii. 32 is curious; she does not appear in Mark xiii. 16 which here is parallel to the Lucan apocalypse. It may be that she was a favourite warning to backsliders in early homiletic. (It is of course possible that Luke xvii. 31 has been transferred from Mark to this apocalypse in order to make room for the Lucan expansion at xxi. 20 ff. by which Mark xiii. 14, the immediately preceding verse, has been expanded into a full-dress prophecy of the destruction of Jerusalem. But the theme may have appeared in both apocalypses; the Lucan and Marcan wording is very similar, but 'roof', 'house', 'go down', 'turn back' were more or less bound to be identical in any version of the saying; but perhaps Luke's version of his source has been coloured by Marcan reminiscences.)

Christian language with which he was familiar in dealing with a specifically Jewish-Christian problem. The kingdom of God as an eschatological force at work on earth exists in virtue of the fact that it is at work in the souls of those who accept it.

[1] My *Hellenistic Elements*, p. 10. The latter point shows the danger of arguing, from the mere fact that we have a bit of typically Lucan Greek prose, that we are dealing with a Lucan addition to the story and not a mere improvement of the wording of his sources. No doubt Matt. xxiv. 38 is nearer to the original, but the Lucan description of the days of Noah in xvii. 27 adds nothing. On the other hand the fact that Matthew ignores Lot, while Luke has a clearly recognizable motive for introducing him, makes it reasonably certain that he has here expanded his source.

CHAPTER XVI

A COLLECTION OF PARABLES

The apocalypse of Luke xvii. 20–37 is followed in Luke xviii by the parables of the unjust judge and the Pharisee and the publican. They are classed by Creed as 'two parables on prayer' which is no doubt a true account of their contents. But he notes that 'to each the evangelist has prefixed a slight introduction to explain the purport of the parable', and compares the similar introduction to the parable of the pounds at Luke xix. 11. Now these introductions are unique in the Gospels, except for xiv. 7 where we have a Lucan transition from his inserted miracle to the first 'banquet-saying': here the introduction is more or less necessary. In the two parables under consideration they are not only unnecessary: the introduction to the parable of the unjust judge is definitely inconsistent with the sequel in xviii. 6 ff. which draws an entirely different moral from the parable. In the case of the parable of the pounds (Luke xix. 11–27) the introduction has been added in order to harmonize the parable with the supposed historical setting; if it were not for the enemies who refuse to have this man to reign over us while he is away in a far country, there would be nothing in the story to show that the kingdom of God is not due to appear at any moment. Creed further notes that the spirit of the Lucan addition is the spirit of the conclusion of the parable of the unjust judge. 'Perhaps Luke took both parables from the same source' (p. 232).

In this view he is undoubtedly right; but it raises considerable doubts as to the Lucan authorship of the additions, or at least of some of them. It would seem that he had before him a tract of three parables. Three is a more probable number than two for such a collection; we do indeed find twin-parables in many cases, but those of the unjust judge and the Pharisee and the publican are not genuine twins as are, for instance, those of the lost sheep and the lost coin. Admittedly, they have a general reference to two qualities required in prayer, in one case persistence, in the other humility. But the whole setting and the lesson to be drawn are different. It would appear that the three parables formed a single tract or collection, and that the connexion between them is not one of meaning but of form. The original compiler either found them in oral tradition in their present form, already provided with an introduction and a closing explanation,[1] and for that reason united them, or else in uniting the three parables in a catechetical tract supplied himself the introductory explanation for the benefit of the catechist and his catechumens. It may be noted that he even supplies the rather pointless interjection of xix. 25,[2] in order to conform to the normal practice of ending a collection with a question or an interruption leading up to the final saying of Jesus.

On the other hand, it is unusual for Luke to break up his sources as he would appear to have done here. The parables of the unjust judge and of the Pharisee and the publican are divided from that of the pounds by the Marcan section of Luke xviii. 15–43 and the story of Zacchaeus (xix. 1–10). But the difficulty only arises if it is assumed that the introduction to the parable of the pounds (xix. 11) must emanate from Luke's own head. Creed assumes this in his comment on xix. 27, while inclined to hold that 27 itself, with the amplification of the parable by the theme of the nobleman returning as king to wreak vengeance on his disloyal subjects, is pre-Lucan. If Creed's assumption is rejected, everything falls naturally into place. The most obvious reason for the dislocation of Luke's source is that it mentioned the proximity to Jerusalem, and presumably also the expectation of some of Jesus' entourage that the Parousia was imminent. If, therefore, xix. 11 stood in Luke's source, it was virtually necessary for him to break off after the parable of the unjust judge and to resume his use of Mark until he had brought Jesus through Jericho.

The story of Zacchaeus, regarded by Bultmann as a 'biographical apophthegm' of an ideal type, seems to have been put here by Luke because in his source it was already located at Jericho. It would have been more natural for him to put it elsewhere and to finish off his three parables before putting in a detached story which had

---

[1] For the closing explanation of the parable of the unjust judge see below, p. 114.

[2] The interjection is so gauche that many manuscripts omit it. Creed suggests that the manuscript support is strong enough to justify the view that it is not original. But there was every reason for omitting such an awkward interjection, none for inserting it unless it had always been there.

no necessary home. The story came to Luke from an intensely Aramaizing source (note the Greek of xix. 2). Bultmann may well be right (*Gesch.* pp. 33 f.) in regarding xix. 8 as a Lucan or pre-Lucan addition; it is perhaps most likely that in the original story 9 followed immediately on 6; 7 will then have been a conventional expansion (cf. xv. 2), while 8 is intended to show that the real reason why Jesus went to Zacchaeus' house was that he foreknew that Zacchaeus would be converted. Concerning the historicity or otherwise of the story we have no evidence. Bultmann's view that it is an expansion of the story of the Call of Levi, adapted to days when it was no longer possible simply to 'follow Jesus' in the literal sense, is an interesting speculation, but has no evidence to support it. The lack of strictly logical connexion in the story, which disqualifies it from conforming to the rigidly defined 'apophthegm' type, may be due to the fact that in it is preserved some genuine historical reminiscence.

An alternative explanation for Luke's dislocation of his source is of course quite conceivable, namely that Luke wished to associate the parable of the pounds with the expectation of the Parousia. But it is difficult to see any real reason why he should have done so; he could perfectly well have left the parable where it stood in his source with an 'eschatological' introductory note which did not bring in Jerusalem. On the other hand if Jerusalem stood in his source he may well have thought it desirable to break up his source as he appears to have done. Incidentally it is at least probable that this tract had some good historical information; Creed suggests that Luke derived the imminent expectation of the Parousia among the disciples from the request of the sons of Zebedee, but it is very possible that the source derived it independently from good tradition, since, as we shall see, there is other evidence that it contains highly primitive material which was no longer understood.

If this view is correct, it would follow that the introductions are not Lucan as Smith suggests (p. 153), but drawn by him from an earlier source together with the parables themselves. This suspicion is confirmed by the curious inconsistency already noted between the opening words of xviii. 1 and the quite different lesson drawn from the parable at xviii. 6.[1] The general outlook of the latter

[1] Creed thinks it difficult, in view of the predominance of the thought of ἐκδίκησις in the parable, to detach the conclusion from it. But it would be natural and normal

passage is totally inconsistent with the tenor of the teaching of Jesus; it reflects the same outlook as Rev. vi. 10 and would seem to be the work of a later reviser, possibly Luke himself, writing under the strain of the Asiatic persecution (under Domitian?) which has left its mark on the Apocalypse and the conclusion of I Peter.[1] It may be a saying ascribed to Jesus which Luke or a predecessor inserted in good faith; more probably it is a revision of an original conclusion which ran ὁ δὲ θεὸς οὐ μὴ ἀκούσῃ τὰς προσευχὰς (or δεήσεις) τῶν ἐκλεκτῶν (or δούλων: 'the elect' in the synoptic Gospels are normally eschatological) τῶν βοώντων αὐτῷ ἡμέρας καὶ νυκτός, καὶ μακροθυμεῖ ἐπ' αὐτοῖς; λέγω ὑμῖν ὅτι ἀκούσεται (or ἀκούσει if Luke was not the reviser himself, cf. Blass-Debrunner, N.T. Gramm. §77, appendix, p. 15) αὐτῶν ἐν καίρῳ (?). The amount of alteration required to adapt a promise of answer to persistent prayer into a promise that the end of the persecution and the day of vengeance were at hand was trifling. The view expressed may be sub-Christian; but those who have not suffered persecution cannot afford to be too severe in their judgement of those who have.[2]

The last clause of Luke xviii. 8 is a well-known problem. Creed

for a compiler or expander of such a collection to insert the conclusion simply because it was a saying on ἐκδίκησις without considering whether the thought of the two passages was in any way similar. On the other hand, Luke may have come across the saying and inserted it in order to carry on the theme of the apocalypse which has just preceded it.

[1] We have clear evidence of a complete difference between the persecutions alluded to in the letters to the seven Churches (where the name of Antipas stands out as almost a solitary martyr (ii. 13) and a ten days imprisonment is a temptation from the devil), and the wholesale persecutions implied in vi. 10 ff. where those already slain have only a little time to wait before the full number of 144,000 is reached. No doubt the number of martyrs was really very far short of this number and probably only a few hundreds at the moment; but even apocalyptic mathematics cannot regard one martyr as bringing the number near the required figure (cf. Charles, in *I.C.C. Revelation*, I, 43). Similarly while in the two homilies of I Pet. i. 1–iv. 12 persecution is a nuisance (ii. 12, iii. 13 ff., iv. 4 ff.), in the conclusion 'your adversary the devil is on the prowl all over the world'. But we have no means of dating the persecution in Asia precisely; it was due not, as Charles suggests (*loc. cit.*), to the fact that Domitian insisted on his divinity, which might have affected nobles at Rome, but not the ordinary Asiatic convert, but to the zeal of some particular pro-consul who may have wanted to curry favour with Domitian and therefore taken steps to suppress the Church, using the offering of worship to the Emperor as a test-issue (cf. Kidd, *History of the Church*, I, p. 75).

[2] For the whole passage cf. Smith, *Parables*, pp. 148 ff.

(*ad loc.*) and Smith (p. 152) regard it as an expression of something almost amounting to despair in the face of persecution. This seems most unlikely; the Apocalypse betrays no hint of such an attitude and we have no reason to suppose that other Christian circles were less confident in their deliverance. It seems far more probable that we have here one of the sayings of Jesus which survived because they had somehow found their way into oral tradition and were no longer understood; another striking case is the wistful saying of Luke v. 39 (cf. Vol. 1, p. 15). Both sayings may reflect a half-ironic expression of regret that the hope that the Pharisees would accept the kingdom of heaven had proved illusory. Such sayings would naturally tend to vanish from the tradition after the final breach between the Church and the synagogue; the result is that we have only the 'conflict-stories' of the Marcan tradition and a few isolated sayings, mostly preserved by Luke, to show that there was a time when the breach which led up to the condemnation of Jesus by the Sanhedrin was by no means as inevitable as it appeared in retrospect.[1] The saying has of course no claim to its present position; it is inserted here because it is connected in thought with the cry of the elect for their vindication. Presumably it was inserted by the hand which inserted or revised the preceding verses: but it might be a final addition by Luke if those verses reached him in their present form.

In support of this view it may be noted that the title of 'the Son of Man' occurs in it. The title is Aramaic, even if at times it is a mistranslation of Aramaic.[2] On the other hand the three parables which form this tract are noticeable for the predominance of Hellenistic language and idiom; we may note:

(1) xviii. 2. Cf. the very close parallel from Dion. Halic. *Antt.*

---

[1] 'Faith' in xviii. 8 seems at least as naturally interpreted in the sense of confidence in and fidelity to God, the rabbinical *amunah* or *amanah*, as in Matt. xxiii. 23 (another saying from this stratum), as in the sense of faith in the teaching of the Church (as understood by Creed *ad loc.*). Cf. Acts vi. 5 and xi. 24, where the emphasis is rather on faith as fidelity in God than on the acceptance of the Gospel; the post-Pauline usage is normally coloured by Paul's theology, which again is coloured by his conversion-experience. For the rabbinical conception of 'faith' cf. Moore, *Judaism*, II, 237.

[2] For a discussion of the title cf. T. W. Manson, *The Teaching of Jesus*, pp. 211 ff., and his lecture 'The Son of Man in Daniel, Enoch, and the Gospels', in the *Bulletin of the John Rylands Library*, XXXII (1950), pp. 171–93.

Rom. x, 10, 7: οὔτε θεῖον φοβηθέντες χολὸν οὔτ᾽ ἀνθρωπίνην ἐντρα-πέντες νέμεσιν, quoted by Creed (*ad loc.*). ἐντρέπεσθαι occurs in this sense in Mark xii. 6 and parallels; elsewhere in the New Testament only I Cor. iv. 14, II Thess. iii. 14, Tit. ii. 8, Heb. xii. 9.

(2) ἐκδικεῖν (xviii. 3 and 7) and its derivatives occur once elsewhere in Luke (xxi. 22, a remarkable amplification of the Marcan apocalypse); elsewhere in the New Testament once in Acts, seven times in Paul, once in Hebrews, once in I Peter, and Rev. vi. 10 and xix. 10. Cf. also the remarkable Jewish inscription from Rheneia, quoted by Deissmann, *Licht vom Osten*, pp. 305 ff. (The word is admittedly frequent in LXX.)

(3) ἐπί with accent to denote duration of time (xviii. 4) occurs in the Gospels only here and doubtfully in iv. 25 (W.-H. omit); nine times between Acts xiii. 11 and xxviii. 6, three times in Paul and once in Hebrews.

(4) ὑπωπιάζω (xviii. 5) only here and I Cor. ix. 27 in the New Testament.

(5) ἐξουθενεῖν (xviii. 9) occurs in Mark ix. 12 (in the form ἐξουθενωθῇ, but W.-H. read ἐξουθενηθῇ); elsewhere in the New Testament in Luke xxiii. 11, Acts iv. 11 (from Ps. cxviii. 22, where LXX and Mark xii. 10 and parallels read ἀπεδοκίμασαν); eight times in the Pauline eipstles. (Both forms are common in LXX.)

(6) For εὐχαριστῶ in xviii. 11 cf. my *Hellenistic Elements*, pp. 5 f. For the catalogue of vices in this verse cf. *ibid.* p. 9.

(7) δικαιόω (xviii. 14) occurs in Matt. xi. 19 and xii. 37 in the sense of 'prove right' or 'acquit'. Elsewhere the word is found in Luke vii. 35 (=Matt. xi. 19); also Luke vii. 29 ('pronounced righteous'), x. 29 and xvi. 15 ('acquit'). In Acts xiii. 39 it occurs twice in Luke's summary of the Pauline doctrine of 'justification', which is the meaning here; elsewhere only in the Pauline epistles and the criticism of them in Jas. ii. 21 ff.

(8) παραχρῆμα (xix. 11) appears in Matt. xxi. 19 and 20, where it is due to Matthew's change in the story of the barren fig tree. Elsewhere in the New Testament only in Luke and Acts (sixteen times).

(9) ἀναφαίνεσθαι only here and Acts xxi. 3 in the New Testament. (Classical.)

(10) εὐγενής in xix. 12 appears here and Acts xvii. 11 and I Cor. i. 26.

(11) ὑποστρέφειν (*ibid.*) occurs at Mark xiv. 40 in some manuscripts but as a very doubtful reading, as against πάλιν ἐλθών. Elsewhere in the New Testament in Gal. i. 17, Heb. vii. 1, II Pet. ii. 21; thirty-three times in Luke and Acts.

(12) πραγματεύεσθαι in xix. 13 is good official *koine*, also Xenophon. *Hap. leg.* New Testament, as is the compound form in 15.

(13) ἐπανέρχεσθαι in 15 (only here and Luke x. 35 in the New Testament) is Attic.

(14) προσεργάζεσθαι in 16 appears in Xenophon in this sense (*hap. leg.* New Testament).

(15) αὐστηρός in 21 and 22 is classical and literary *koine* (*hap. leg.* New Testament).

(16) τράπεζα in 23 (=bank) is classical and good *koine*. (Not elsewhere in this sense in the New Testament.)

(17) κατασφάττειν. *Hap. leg.* New Testament, classical.

On the other hand we have in xviii. 6 the Hebraism ὁ κρίτης τῆς ἀδικίας, cf. above, p. 94. But the examples given by Blass-Debrunner (*N.T. Gramm.* § 165) show that the usage is pre-eminently a Paulinism (Rom. i. 26, vi. 6, vii. 24, Phil. iii. 21, etc.). προσθεὶς εἶπεν in xix. 11 is a Hebraism but common in Luke (cf. Creed *ad loc.*). πλήν in 27 is not a word which Luke uses where it is not in his sources; but Paul has no objection to it (I Cor. xi. 11, Phil. iii. 16, iv. 14; cf. *Hellenistic Elements*, p. 12). ἴσθι ἐξουσίαν ἔχων in xix. 17 is hard to defend (cf. above, p. 78): Luke retains it from his sources, but does not use it himself; Paul has no objection to it (cf. Blass-Debrunner, § 353).

It would seem that the triad of parables in this collection has undergone a considerable revision in the course of transmission. In the parable of the unjust judge this affects the substance as well as the language: the parable of the Pharisee and publican shows linguistic revision only. It is the parable of the pounds that shows the most drastic revision. The rise of Gnosticism made it necessary to rewrite the original parable of the talents; each servant had to receive the same initial trust, so as to avoid any appearance of support in the teaching of Jesus for the Gnostic doctrine of three different types of mankind (cf. *Gentiles*, p. 149, n. 5). The original parable as in the Matthean version had only three slaves; we hear nothing in Luke of the seven who are left over when the nobleman has made up his accounts with the first three; but the reviser had the number ten running in his head, apparently because the first servant of the original received five talents and gained another five, and so he started with ten slaves and ten minae. This was probably the last emendation. Earlier changes had transferred the parable from its original purpose as a warning to the scribes and Pharisees into a warning to Christians in general by the adding of the saying of Matt. xxv. 28 f.=Luke xix. 26, and had altered the original warning to the leaders of the Jews that they had neglected to use the Torah rightly into an apocalyptic warning of the Lord's return.[1] By the time the parable reached Luke it had been further developed; the story of Archelaus and the destruction of Jerusalem had suggested a new feature, namely the rejection of the Jews manifested in the destruction of Jerusalem, the fall of the city being regarded as a sign of the imminence of the Parousia and so closely associated with it that the two events could be treated as one; we find them so associated in Luke's version of the Marcan apocalypse.[2] This element, i.e. the receiving of the kingdom and retribution for the dissidents (12 b, 14–15 a, and 27), would seem to have been added before the story reached Luke, since apart from them there would be no point in dislocating the source and putting the parable after the Marcan section xviii. 15–43 and the story of Zacchaeus. As has been noted above, the source may have had good information as to the disciples' expectation of the Parousia at the time of Jesus' entry into Jerusalem; it is possible that this was the reason for the amplification of the parable by the addition of the rejection of the Jews to the warning against the failure to use God's gifts; this had originally been addressed to them but had by now been changed into a warning to the lukewarm Christian. This addition would seem to be pre-Lucan. The interruption of *v.* 25 is proper for the ending of such a collection of parables; its awkwardness in its present form is probably simply due to a piece

---

[1] For this account of the development of the parable cf. Smith, *Parables*, pp. 168 f.

[2] Luke xxi. 24 leaves an interval 'until the times of the Gentiles are fulfilled' during which Jerusalem is to be trodden underfoot by the Gentiles. But the clause may be itself an attempt to explain the delay between the fall of the city and the final distress which precedes the appearance of the Son of Man; otherwise it is to be presumed that the fulfilment of the times of the Gentiles (as determined by the stars?) is expected to follow very shortly, as in Mark xiii. It follows shortly after the setting up of the abomination of desolation.

of clumsiness by the reviser who added verse 27 in the margin of the tract, or possibly to a piece of clumsiness on Luke's part in crossing out εἶπεν δὲ (sc. ὁ κύριος) ἀμήν when he simply meant to delete ἀμήν before λέγω ὑμῖν.

The whole tract would seem to have come to Luke through a Hellenistic and probably Pauline medium. This would explain the linguistic phenomena; the number of classical words is unusually high and there seems no reason why Luke should have done so much rewriting to his source at this point. It is of course possible that some are due to him; but it seems likely that his source had been to some extent hellenized before it reached him, though it also contained Semitisms and Greek phrases which he normally avoids. In any case the fact that the parable of the pounds came to him in the last resort from the same source as Matthew's parable of the talents, though by a widely different line of transmission, does not prove that we are dealing with Lucan inventions.

PART III

THE SOURCES OF MATTHEW

CHAPTER XVII

THE BIRTH OF JESUS AND THE FULFILMENT OF PROPHECY

It has already been noted that in the Sermon on the Mount we have evidence that Matthew is incorporating two sources quite apart from the matter which he draws from his Q stratum, a summary of the new Torah with three sayings on the great Christian duties, and a bitterly anti-Gentile source, which reappears at xviii. 15 ff. The first evangelist's habit of breaking up his material and rearranging it so as to make an artistic whole makes it peculiarly difficult to be sure whether he is using isolated stories and sayings which came to him in what he regarded as reliable tradition. Nor is it always clear whether he is drawing on sources common to himself and Luke, but heavily rewritten by both, or whether both are using independent versions of the same material. For instance, we have seen that the parables of the pounds and the talents were originally the same, but it is probable that they had developed many of their present differences before they reached the evangelists. It is even harder to say what is the relation of Luke xiii. 25 to the parable of the ten virgins (cf. above, p. 80).

None the less there are certain collections of incidents or sayings which are fairly clearly drawn by Matthew from a source, of which at least a large part has survived in something like its original form. The first case, and one of the most striking, is the infancy narrative of Matthew. Here we have a set of five stories, each with a marked unity of structure, which is even more clearly marked if, as will be suggested below, the Magi are an intrusion from another source. Each story is woven round a *testimonium* from the Old Testament; and each *testimonium*, except for i. 23, appears to be drawn not from the LXX or some recension of it, as is usual with Matthew, but from some quite independent version which is not very close to the Masoretic text in its present form.[1] Matt. ii. 23 remains a puzzle; nothing like it can be found in any version of the Old Testament.

[1] Cf. Kilpatrick, *Origins*, p. 54.

The original substratum of the source would appear to be the three Joseph stories (i. 18–25, ii. 13–15, 19–23). The first of these in its present form has undergone revision; as it stands it does not describe the birth of Jesus but explains why Joseph did not divorce Mary (cf. Kilpatrick, *loc. cit.*). It may be suggested that in the original form 18 was the introduction to the story, while 19 is a later addition, introduced by Matthew or an earlier reviser to meet the second point. The first story then opened with some such phrase as ταραχθέντος δὲ τοῦ Ἰωσήφ. With this reconstruction we get the following scheme:

(1) An opening genitive absolute.
(2) 'Behold, an angel of the Lord appears to Joseph in a dream.'
(3) 'And Joseph, when he awoke', proceeded to obey the angel.
(4) 'That it might be fulfilled which was spoken by the Lord to the prophet' (slightly modified in ii. 23) with the appropriate *testimonium*.

In the original, ii. 13 was introduced not with the words 'And when they had departed', but with 'When Jesus was born in Bethlehem in the days of Herod the king'. In the last story there has been an expansion which, as it stands, gives an awkward double motive for Joseph's withdrawal to Nazareth, his fear of Archelaus and the warning of the angel. It may be suspected that one, and possibly both, of the motives represent later expansion of the original story, which simply told that he went to the land of Israel to a city called Nazareth, in order that the prophecy might be fulfilled.[1]

It would seem that this group of prophecies was expanded by the introduction of the Herod incidents, which enabled Matthew to surround the birth of Jesus with five prophecies, his favourite number. It should be observed that the Magi do not fulfil any prophecy, although such prophecies could easily have been found.[2] The length of the story of Matt. ii. 2 and the lack of unity of time and place suggest that it is a conflation of two earlier stories, one of which simply described the visit of the wise men, while the other

---

[1] For the difficulties of ii. 23 cf. Allen *ad loc.*

[2] Justin (*Dial.* 77–8) uses Isa. viii. 4 to prove that Ps. lxxii is addressed to Jesus not to Hezekiah, who did not receive the 'power of Damascus and the spoils of Syria' before he was old enough to say 'My father or my mother'. Cf. Tert. *adv. Marc.* III, 13, *adv. Jud.* IX, where Zech. xv. 14 is also used as a *testimonium*.

described how a star appeared in Jerusalem; its appearance led Herod to summon the rulers of the Jews, who told him on the strength of Mic. v. 1 that the Christ would be born in Bethlehem. Accordingly Herod ordered the massacre of the innocents. The story of the Magi has been so interwoven with the consultation of the rulers of the Jews by Herod that the two strands cannot be separated; in 13 ἀναχωρησάντων δὲ αὐτῶν and in 16 ἰδὼν ὅτι ἐνεπαίχθη ὑπὸ τῶν μάγων have been inserted by Matthew to secure the continuity of his story. The source from which the prophecies came would seem to have been a collection of proof-texts, which expanded with the lapse of time as Christian ingenuity was able either to discover prophecies which could be read into the story or to expand the story with incidents which could be claimed as fulfilments of prophecy. A subsidiary motive of the collection seems to have been the drawing out of the parallelism between the birth of Jesus and that of Moses, especially prominent in the massacre of the innocents and perhaps in that it is Egypt which saves the child's life. This, however, is a secondary theme, and the fact that the typological correspondence is not more complete suggests that it has been superimposed upon the infancy narrative at a stage in its growth which is not primary. It should, however, be observed that the core of the story goes back to a tradition which is old enough for the Lucan version of the birth and infancy to have been developed along entirely different lines before it reached the evangelist.[1] How far Matthew has expanded the sources himself it is impossible to say. The wording of the whole passage is in general agreement with the Matthean style, but there is no reason to suppose that he is responsible for more than his normal amount of editorial revision.

It is hard to agree with Kilpatrick (pp. 52–3) that there is an extraordinary or excessive use of Matthean expressions in Matt. i. 18–25 or in Matt. ii. An expression can only be called Matthean if there is a very marked difference in the use of it between Matthew on the one hand and Mark and Luke on the other. For a difference to be significant I should suppose that we ought to find Matthew using it about twice as often as the others, and that where a word occurs less than ten times there should be a clear majority of five in Matthew, except perhaps where a word is peculiar

---

[1] Cf. Kilpatrick, *Origins*, p. 54.

to him and the other evangelists use a different word. An examination of Moulton and Geden's concordance gives the following results:

In Matt. i. 18–25: οὕτως Mt. 33, Mk. 10, Lk. 21; μή with aorist subjunctive Mt. 33, Mk. 15, Lk. 16; θέλειν Mt. 42, Mk. 25, Lk. 28; ἐνθυμεῖσθαι Mt. 2, Mk. 0, Lk. 0; ἰδού Mt. 61, Mk. 8, Lk. 57; ἄγγελος κυρίου Mt. 4, Mk. 0, Lk. 2 (all in the infancy story; 4 times in Acts); κατ' ὄναρ Mt. 6, Mk. 0, Lk. 0 (of Matthew's 6, 5 are in Matt. i–ii); φαίνεσθαι Mt. 14, Mk. 2, Lk. 2; φοβεῖσθαι Mt. 18, Mk. 12, Lk. 22; παραλαμβάνειν Mt. 16, Mk. 6, Lk. 7 (of Matthew's 16, 6 are in Matt. i–ii; outside the infancy narrative the difference is not significant); τοῦτο δὲ ὅλον γέγονεν Mt. 3, Mk. 0, Lk. 0, and ἵνα πληρωθῇ Mt. 10, Mk. 0, Lk. 0 (including the use of ὅπως—but is this Matthew or his collection of *testimonia*?); ἕως Mt. 27, Mk. 9, Lk. 12; ἐγείρειν Mt. 35, Mk. 18, Lk. 18 (here 5 are in Matt. i–ii).

In Matt. ii: ἀνατολαί Mt. 3, Mk. 0, Lk. 1 (if the singular is included, Mt. 5 (3 in Matt. ii), Lk. 2); παραγίνεσθαι Mt. 3, Mk. 1, Lk. 8; προσκυνεῖν Mt. 12, Mk. 2, Lk. 3; συνάγειν Mt. 24, Mk. 5, Lk. 6; λαός Mt. 14, Mk. 3, Lk. 37; (λαός after ἀρχιερεῖς καὶ γραμματεῖς, Mt. 5, Mk. 0, Lk. 10); καλεῖν Mt. 25, Mk. 4, Lk. 43; πέμπειν Mt. 4, Mk. 1, Lk. 10; πορεύεσθαι Mt. 28, Mk. 1, Lk. 49; ἐξετάζειν Mt. 2, Mk. 0, Lk. 0; εὑρίσκειν Mt. 27, Mk. 10, Lk. 47; ἀπαγγέλλειν Mt. 8, Mk. 3, Lk. 11; ἐπάνω Mt. 8, Mk. 1, Lk. 5; χαίρειν Mt. 6, Mk. 2, Lk. 12; χαρά Mt. 6, Mk. 1, Lk. 8; σφόδρα Mt. 7, Mk. 1, Lk. 1; πίπτειν Mt. 18, Mk. 8, Lk. 17; προσφέρειν Mt. 15, Mk. 3, Lk. 4; χρύσος Mt. 4, Mk. 0, Lk. 0; δι' ὁδοῦ Mt. 2, Mk. 0, Lk. 0 (but in Matt. viii. 28 διὰ τῆς ὁδοῦ); ἀναχωρεῖν Mt. 10, Mk. 1, Lk. 0; ἀνοίγειν Mt. 11, Mk. 1, Lk. 7; θησαυρός Mt. 4, Mk. 1, Lk. 4; νυκτός Mt. 3, Mk. 0, Lk. 1; ἐκεῖ Mt. 29, Mk. 11, Lk. 16; ἕως ἄν Mt. 9, Mk. 2, Lk. 3; τότε Mt. 91, Mk. 6, Lk. 15; τελευτᾶν Mt. 4, Mk. 2, Lk. 1; τὰ μέρη Mt. 3, Mk. 1, Lk. 0 (4 times in Acts); κατοικεῖν Mt. 4, Mk. 0, Lk. 2 (20 times in Acts).

In evaluating the evidential significance of these figures it must be remembered that on account of the brevity of the Second Gospel the Marcan figures are inevitably smaller, and in comparing Matthew with Luke that Luke has a better sense of Greek and frequently changes his source; thus at Matt. viii. 15 we have ἠγέρθη from the ἤγειρεν of Mark i. 31, while Luke iv. 39 reads ἀναστᾶσα. Five uses of the word come in these two chapters and cannot be adduced as evidence without a *petitio principii*, while three more come in the Matthean version of the Passion story at xxvii. 52 and 63 f. Similarly if we deduct the uses of παραλαμβάνειν in these two chapters there is no significant difference between Matthew and the rest. Again θησαυρός ii. 11 owes its greater frequency in Matthew to two sayings peculiar to Matthew (xiii. 44 and 52) and to the

Semitic parallelism of Matt. vi. 19 ff. and xii. 35, as a result of which Matthew has the word six times as against Luke's three.

If we deduct the words which are more frequent in Luke than in Matthew and those where the difference is not significant, it would seem that of those left οὕτως is a very doubtful case: Luke has κατὰ τὰ αὐτά at vi. 20= Matt. v. 12, ὁμοίως at vi. 31=Matt. vii. 12; Matt. iii. 15 and xiii. 40 and 49 have no parallels: the word is bound to occur frequently unless deliberately replaced by an equivalent. φαίνεσθαι can hardly be claimed since it appears 4 times in cc. i and ii and three times in the tract from which Matt. vi. 5, 16 and 18 are drawn; τοῦτο δὲ...ἵνα πληρωθῇ is a formula of quotation which may be due to Matthew, but equally may be due to his source; προσφέρω is Matthean, but it is usually employed by him in revising his sources (iv. 24=Mark iii. 10, viii. 16=Mark i. 32, ix. 2= Mark ii. 3, ix. 32 with its doublet xii. 22=Luke xi. 14 and are from the Q stratum; xiv. 35=Mark vi. 55, xvii. 16=Mark ix. 18, xxii. 19=Mark xii. 16, xxv. 20=Luke xxi. 16 from the Q stratum; συνάγειν apart from its peculiar use in xxv. 35, 38 and 43 (=כום?; cf. Allen *ad loc.*) owes its predominance to Matthew's use of it in editing Mark.

Thus the really significant words, such as προσφέρειν and συνάγειν, to which we may add προσκυνεῖν, ἕως (?), τότε and σφόδρα, are clear evidence that Matthew has submitted these chapters to an editorial revision similar to that which we find in the rest of the Gospel, a fact of which there was never any doubt. They provide no evidence which would justify us in holding that these sections come from his own pen, any more than the appearance of similar words in passages which he has drawn from Mark or his Q stratum.

The view that Matthew is not responsible for more than his normal amount of editorial revision in the infancy narrative is borne out by the fact that in i. 20, 22, 24, ii. 13 and 19, God is described as κύριος (in i. 23 θεός was necessary and inevitable). This usage is not Matthean; elsewhere God is only referred to as κύριος in quotations from the Old Testament, except for xxviii. 2. Probably the phrase ἄγγελος κυρίου 'the angel of the Lord' is Jewish-Christian Greek, though in xxii. 20 there is strong support for 'angels of God'. In xxii. 31 we have 'by God' in a passage where Matthew is rewriting Mark so drastically that he could perfectly well have substituted κύριος for θεός if he had preferred it in his Old Testament quotations. Since, however, he is quoting an E not a J passage he allows θεός to remain. The steady preference for κύριος in the probably editorial phrase, 'that it might be fulfilled which was spoken by the Lord through the prophet', confirms the view that we are dealing in these chapters not with a Matthean composition but with an older narrative, based on the fulfilment of prophecy in the birth of Jesus, which had already assumed a fixed form before it came to Matthew. It would seem that this narrative had already been expanded by the addition of the Herod prophecies to the Joseph group; it is possible that Matthew himself is responsible for the introduction of the wise men, who fulfil no prophecy and disturb the general structure of the source. This is exactly how he has treated his source at v. 21 ff., preserving the original so that the structure is clearly distinguishable, yet modifying it by the introduction of extraneous matter (cf. above, p. 20).[1]

The *testimonia* of the infancy narrative are, however, only part of a larger group of fulfilments of prophecy in Matthew all of which are introduced with the common 'That it might be fulfilled which was spoken by the Lord through the prophet', or a slight variation of that form. These are iv. 14 ff., viii. 17, xii. 17 ff., xiii. 35, xxi. 4 f. and xxvii. 9. This group of quotations agrees with those of the infancy narrative in differing widely from the LXX.[2] The six instances fall into two distinct groups. The first four are concerned to show that the general outlines of the ministry of Jesus were the fulfilment of prophecy. Its location in Galilee (iv. 14 f.) fulfils Isa. viii. 23; the healings (viii. 17) fulfil Isa. liii. 4; Jesus' refusal to court publicity (xii. 17) fulfils Isa. xlii. 1 ff.; his parables (xiii. 35) fulfil Ps. lxxviii. 2. On the other hand xxi. 4 f. gives a version of the triumphal entry crudely modified by the introduction of the ass's colt in order to find a fulfilment of Zech. ix. 9 (cf. Vol. 1, p. 77), while xxvii. 9 has led to the transformation of the prophecy of Zech. xi. 12 (wrongly assigned to Jeremiah) into the story of the use of

[1] In general I agree with Kilpatrick's view (p. 55) that the main lines of the stories and the quotations were already fixed when they came to the evangelist. But I cannot see that he had rewritten them noticeably more than he has rewritten Mark and his Q material. It is quite possible that he was the first to reduce them to writing, but they were already fixed in a stereotyped oral form, even if they had never been written down before. It is, of course, possible that Matt. i. 21 was originally a quotation from Ps. cxxx. 8; but it is not introduced as one, and its resemblance to Ps. cxxx. 8 and its differences from the LXX and the Masoretic text may indicate that it is merely an unconscious assimilation of the story to Biblical language.

[2] For the details cf. Kilpatrick, pp. 57 and 93 ff.

Judas' thirty pieces of silver to buy the potter's field. It seems very unlikely that all these come from a single collection in the first instance, but it seems perfectly reasonable to suppose that at some period it had been thought worth while to collect a set of *testimonia* which would prove that the general outlines of the ministry of Jesus (as summarized for instance in Mark's Twelve-source) were foretold by the prophets. Once such collections came into existence, they would inevitably grow as they attracted to themselves, snowball-fashion, other prophecies whose fulfilment could be read into the Gospel story (or which could be changed from prophecies into incidents which ought to have occurred and therefore must have occurred). I am inclined to suggest that Matthew had before him a collection of *testimonia* comprising the first four prophecies of this group, and that he added the other two from some other source, which may have been oral tradition (cf. Kilpatrick, p. 46). It is to be presumed that the introductory formula became stereotyped at a fairly early stage, though it is possible that Matthew has introduced it where he did not find it in his sources; this seems particularly likely to have happened at xxi. 4 and xxvii. 9. The first four may well only have been part of a larger whole, the rest of which is lost; but it is hardly likely that they were originally part of the same collection as the infancy prophecies, though the two collections may conceivably have been united before they reached Matthew. It might indeed be supposed that the recognition of individual incidents (whether real or imagined) as the fulfilment of prophecy would be more primitive than the attempt to read the general course of the ministry of Jesus as such a fulfilment, and that in consequence Matt. xxi. 4 f. and xxvii. 9 ff. are more primitive than the first four. This rests on a complete misapprehension of the actual development of the argument from prophecy. The unknown compiler of the collection from which the first four prophecies of this group are drawn was concerned to describe the general features of the ministry of Jesus and to see in them a fulfilment of the Old Testament. The result was that he produced a collection which had no apologetic value for those who wanted to find in the incidents of the Gospels, especially the Nativity and Passion, dramatic fulfilments of particular prophecies; the later Christian writers are concerned to find *testimonia* of this dramatic type, while the more general fulfilments are ignored.[1] The appearance of this collection is not without interest as suggesting a general 'biographical' interest in the career of Jesus as the fulfilment of prophecy, which was swamped by the later desire for more detailed prophecies or the growing interest in typology.

[1] Apart from the interest of the *Epistle of Barnabas* in the details of the Passion (*Ep. Barn.* v. 2, 12 ff., and vi) and the use of Isa. liii of the Passion in Clem. Rom. *Ep. ad Cor.* xvi the Apostolic Fathers have little to say on the relation of prophecy to the ministry of Jesus; but it must be remembered that Hermas and Ignatius are practically ignorant of the Old Testament. In the second and third centuries we naturally find references to Isa. liii. 4 quoted (Iren. *Haer.* IV, 33, 11; but Irenaeus is far more interested in showing that Hab. iii. 3 foretells the birth of Jesus at Bethlehem, and Amos viii. 9 f. and Jer. xv. 9 the eclipse which accompanied the Crucifixion). Justin does not seem to quote this particular verse, though he uses Isa. liii frequently; Tertullian, *adv. Marc.* III, 17, uses it as a prophecy of Jesus' miracles of healing in a running exposition of the whole chapter; cf. IV. 8. Isa. xlii. 2 ff.=Matt. xii. 19 ff. is used by Tert. *adv. Jud.* IX to prove that Jesus is the Messiah; cf. *adv. Marc.* III, 17 and 21; and IV, 23 it is used to prove that the God of the Old Testament and the prophets is a God of mercy and not simply of justice; but this is not the Matthean use. The only use of Isa. ix. 1–2=Matt. iv. 15–16 that I can trace is *Didascalia*, v, 16, 2 (p. 186, Connolly), where, however, it foretells the conversion of some of the Jews and appeals to such converts to pray for their brethren, and is not, as in Matthew, a *testimonium* to prove that Jesus is the Messiah. I cannot trace any use of Ps. lxxviii. 2=Matt. xiii. 35, though Clem. Alex. uses the words of Matt. xiii. 34 to justify his belief of an element of mystery in the Christian tradition. Tert. *adv. Marc.* V, 11 uses it, but simply to prove that Jesus uses the methods of the Old Testament writers. On the other hand Isa. vi. 9=Mark xiii. 11 ff. is a favourite, not because it is a prophecy of his use of parables, but because it foretells the rejection of the Jews (Iren. *Haer.* IV, 29, 1, Tert. *adv. Marc.* III, 6, *Didasc.* III, 6, 6 (= *Const. Apost.* III, 6, 5), VI, 16, 11, *Const. Apost.* V, 16, 4). As against this Zech. ix. 9 (=Matt. xxi. 4) is quoted by Justin, *Apol.* I, 35, 76 C, *Dial.* 53, 272 D, Iren. *Haer.* IV, 33, 1, and is slipped into what is really a collection of typology in *Const. Apost.* V, 20, 10 and is given an allegorical interpretation in Clem. Alex. *Paed.* I, 5, 15 (106 P). Curiously enough Tertullian does not seem to use it. For the use of details of the Gospel narrative to prove the fulfilment of prophecy, especially in the Passion, cf. Justin, *Apol.* I, 34 ff. (75 D), *Dial.* 97 ff. (32 A) where we have an elaborate exposition of Ps. xxii on these lines. Cf. Iren. *Haer.* IV, 33, 11 ff., referred to above. In Tert. *adv. Jud.* VII ff. we have the familiar string of *testimonia* drawn from the incidents of the Gospels expanded by a chronological calculation to prove that Daniel ix exactly fits the date of the first coming of Christ.

CHAPTER XVIII

THE FIRST COLLECTION OF PARABLES

It has already been noticed (above, p. 25) that in the Sermon on the Mount we have one collection of sayings, dealing with the new Torah in respect of three commandments and the three Christian duties of prayer, fasting, and almsgiving. Such a collection can hardly have stood by itself; there must originally have been three triads. The sayings that follow, though they form a group of three sayings on treasures, the single eye and serving two masters, will not fill the gap. In the first place they all deal with the same theme, the disciple's attitude to riches; in the second place Matt. vi. 24, on serving God and Mammon, always belonged to the discourse on worldly cares which follows (cf. above, p. 28). It does not, however, seem to be possible to recover the last triad, probably for the reason that Matthew, who has spoilt the original symmetry of the sayings of this source by expanding it from his Q material, has worked the last triad up with other material till it is no longer recognizable.

It would indeed be possible to hold that the last triad was the three parables of Matt. xiii. 44–50. It will be seen that they form a well-marked group. This is, however, not very likely. The theme of these parables is the kingdom of heaven, a theme which does not appear in the rest of the source. Nor have the other sayings a parabolic character, except in so far as any epigrammatic saying can be described as a *mashal*. The objection is not entirely fatal, since it is possible that the whole collection gave a sort of summary of the teaching of Jesus, and that the parables were included to show the part played in it by parables. But this explanation, while not entirely impossible, seems very unlikely.

Nevertheless, the parables of Matt. xiii. 44–50 seem to form a fragment of a collection. They are distinguished sharply from the group which precedes them by the fact that they lack a formal introduction such as marks the parables of the tares, the mustard seed and the leaven. The actual form of the introduction in Matt. xiii. 24, 31 and 33 is Matthean, but a comparison with Mark iv. 30 and Luke xiii. 20 shows that the last two circulated in the tradition with a more formal introduction than we find in the three of the latter group.

As regards the former group it has already been noted that the parable of the mustard seed circulated in two versions which Matthew has combined (see above, p. 70). It is probable that the parable of the tares had become attached to these two in the tradition from which Matthew derived them; there seems no reason for its omission by Luke, but this is not a decisive argument. In any case the parable would seem to have been heavily edited in the interests of the explanation; 'enemies' are not needed to sow tares in a field, and labourers would hardly be so foolish as to ask the question of xiii. 27. It would seem that the original parable told how the farmer sowed good seed, but the tares sprang up with it; the servants asked whether to hoe the field and were told to wait till the harvest for fear of damaging the crop; the omission of 25, 27, 28a and all but the opening clause of 30, with a consequential alteration of αὐτῷ into τῷ οἰκοδεσπότῃ in 28b, gives the original form.[1] The parable will then have resembled the parables of the seed growing secretly and of the mustard seed pretty closely in form and structure, and it is perhaps worth asking whether it is not a substitute for the parable of the seed growing secretly of Mark iv. 26 ff. Clearly neither Matthew nor Luke understood it; and if, as has been suggested, it referred originally to the Zealot movement, there was plenty of time for its meaning to be forgotten even before it reached Mark. I am inclined to suggest that the Marcan parable had been recast in the shorter form of the parable of the tares suggested above, and was current in oral tradition; Matthew inserted it here with his own eschatological improvements and his own explanation. But it is

---

[1] I owe this explanation to a discussion at Professor Dodd's seminar, but I fear I cannot say exactly which of the members contributed most to the solution. For an explanation cf. Dodd, *Parables*, pp. 183 ff. But I am not entirely clear that the thought of good and evil being mixed in the kingdom of God need be secondary. Even in the lifetime of Jesus it is to be presumed that there was need of explanation for the mixture of good and bad among his followers who constituted the kingdom at the moment; we must allow for the probability that there were apparently enthusiastic followers who fell away rapidly.

possible that both these stages are older than Matthew, and quite possible that the parable of the tares has no connexion with that of the seed growing secretly of Mark iv. 26 ff.

The three parables of the second group (Matt. xiii. 44–50) are again closely alike in form and content. The Dragnet in its original form (cf. Dodd, *Parables*, p. 189) originally stopped at xiii. 48 and thus falls into line with the two that preceded it; the three would seem to have been combined before they reached Matthew in view of their striking similarity of form; once again Matthew has spoilt it by his insertion of 49 f. It is scarcely possible that they ever formed a complete tract, whether written or oral, in view of their brevity, but there seems no means of saying whether any more of this source has been preserved. It is possible that they came to Matthew combined with the two parables of xiii. 31–3, but the difference in the formulas of introduction tells against such a view. Moreover, the former pair came to Luke in the same form, while there is no reason why he should have omitted the latter three if he knew of them. The latter objection need not be fatal, since short parables of this kind might easily be combined into various groups without any change of wording; but on the whole it is more probable that the three came to Matthew with other elements, which he has either omitted or worked in elsewhere. It must be remembered that there may quite well have been longer and shorter versions of the same parable in circulation, and that Matthew may have omitted, for example, a shorter version of the parable of the ten virgins from this collection because he preferred the fuller version which came to him through another channel (cf. above, p. 80).

The saying of Matt. xiii. 51 f. is interesting and has high claims to authenticity. Its preservation may be due to the same motives as have led Matthew to include the curious saying of v. 19 (cf. p. 19). The saying that the scribe who is instructed in the kingdom of heaven brings out of his treasures things new and old may very well have been preserved in the tradition because it could be interpreted as a criticism of the Pauline point of view; the Christian scribe has both new and old, not merely new. But it may well be doubted whether the saying would ever have been coined by any Jewish-Christian circle, since the scribes and Pharisees are always the conventional opponents of Jesus and his followers, especially in Matthew. It may well have been uttered by Jesus on the occasion of the acceptance of his teaching by a disciple of some leading rabbi at a period when he still hoped to be accepted by the religious leaders of the nation, and so been preserved in a crystallized form after the breach between the Church and the synagogue had become final and irrevocable and the Pharisees had been made into the villains of the whole story.[1]

[1] Cf. Kilpatrick, *Origins*, p. 121.

CHAPTER XIX

A 'CHURCH ORDER' AND
A COLLECTION OF PARABLES

At Matt. xviii. 15 ff. we have an interesting fragment, running as far as xviii. 22. It deals for the most part with forgiveness, and shows the first beginnings of a penitential system within the Church, though it deals only with sins committed by one brother against another.[1] But the authority given to the Church to 'bind and loose'[2] has led to the insertion of the saying of 19 f.: the insertion may be due to Matthew but may well have stood in his source. The 'Verily I say unto you' and 'Again I say unto you' of 18 and 19 may well be Matthew's revision of 'Jesus also said' of his source.

The sayings seem to be drawn from a collection which Matthew has used already, the bitterly anti-Gentile source from which v. 47 and vi. 7 are drawn (cf. above, p. 33). It might seem inconsistent with the outlook of such a source to combine the wide charity towards 'brethren' of v. 47 ff. and xviii. 21 with the hatred of Gentiles which characterizes it; unfortunately the history of religion shows that the apparent inconsistency of a close love for brethren within the community with hatred of all outside it is more or less normal, especially in small minority groups which are liable to persecution. Naturally we are unable to say how much other material in Matthew may be drawn from this source, since we can only isolate it where it gives expression to its hatred of Gentiles and publicans. So far as we can trace it, it would seem to have been a Manual of Discipline for Jewish Christians not dissimilar to the Zadokite fragment.[3] It does not appear to have dealt with sins except those against the brethren; it may be presumed that the capital sins of

---

[1] On Matt. xviii. 15 cf. D. Daube, 'κερδαίνω as a missionary term', *Harv. Th. Rev.* XI (1947), pp. 109–20, and his remarks in *Studia Theologica*, I (1947), at p. 168.

[2] For 'binding and loosing' as covering the two senses of forbidding or declaring permissible and excluding from or readmitting to the synagogue, cf. Str.-B. on Matt. xvi. 19.

[3] Cf. especially ix. 29–x. 6 (in R. H. Charles, *Apocr. and Pseud.* II, pp. 820 ff.).

apostasy, idolatry, murder and adultery were regarded as outside the pale of forgiveness.[1]

It is possible that Peter's question and Jesus' reply (Matt. xviii. 21–2) formed the conclusion of this collection; a question by a by-stander and a reply of a striking character are the normal endings for these tracts. In itself the question and answer raise an interesting point. It has been noted above that the Matthean saying is a variant of the forgiveness 'unto seven times' of Luke xvii. 4. Whether the variation is due to Matthew or his source cannot be said; in any case it casts an interesting light on the attitude of early Jewish Christianity to the sayings of Jesus. For it might conceivably be possible for a brother to inflict injury or annoyance as much as seven times in a day; it would seem that there was a danger that the offended brother would suppose that on the eighth offence he could refuse forgive-ness, and the saying has been altered so as to provide a total which could hardly be reached and certainly could not be counted with precise accuracy. It is possible that the parable of the unmerciful debtor (Matt. xviii. 23–35) had been added to the collection of sayings common to Luke and Matthew in the form in which it reached Matthew, though not in the form in which it reached Luke; but this is hardly probable. It is more likely that the parable formed one of a group of three parables, which Matthew has broken up, the other two being those of the labourers in the vineyard (xx. 1 ff.) and of the ten virgins (xxv. 1 ff.).

These three parables have a formal unity of subject in so far as they all open with the formula 'The kingdom of heaven is like unto' a person or group of persons; in the case of the ten virgins the future 'shall be like unto' is necessitated by the fact that the parable, what-ever its original meaning may have been (for this cf. Dodd, *Parables*, pp. 171 ff.), has become a picture of the Last Judgement. The parable of the unmerciful servant is concerned with the present con-duct of those who claim to be members of the kingdom, and that of the labourers in the vineyard deals, at any rate in its present form, with the position of the Church as the heir of the world-ages which have gone before.[2] In its original form it dealt with the kingdom of

---

[1] Cf. Watkins, *A History of Penance*, I, p. 14.

[2] For the five periods of the parable cf. the five world-ages before the Messianic age (which in the parable has now begun), also Charles, *Apocr. and Pseud.* II, p. 451,

God as the sphere in which the labourer receives his reward, that is, the kingdom to be established at the end of time, not the kingdom as a present fact. But to a compiler of parables the verbal identity would be enough. The parables have the further peculiarity that they all are introduced to illustrate some particular piece of teaching which is repeated at the end in a similar form. In xviii. 23 ff. this is obscured by the fact that the lesson, that men must forgive their brethren if they would be forgiven by God, has been replaced by the saying of 22 on forgiving unto seventy times seven; presumably in the original it was introduced by some such words as those of Matt. vi. 14 f. In xx. 1 ff. the parable of the labourers in the vineyard is introduced by 'Many that are first shall be last and the last shall be first'. At xxv. 1 ff. we have no such introduction, but here the introduction could be omitted since at xxiv. 42 Matthew has the almost identical saying 'watch therefore, for ye know not at what hour your Lord cometh' from Mark xiii. 35 a, only separated from the parable of the ten virgins by the section 43–51 which he draws from his Q material (=Luke xii. 39–46).

It might indeed be urged that the concluding aphorisms are simply added by Matthew at xviii. 35 and xxv. 13; he has added a very inappropriate one at xxii. 14 (cf. Smith, p. 206). On the other hand we have already discovered a comparable tract of three parables, with an introduction which points forward to the moral and a con-

and *Gentiles*, pp. 6 ff. I cannot doubt that Irenaeus, *adv. Haer.* IV, 36, 7, is right in seeing that the five callings are the five world-ages, though he is concerned to show that the parable proves that the God of the Old Testament is the same as the God of the New. Origen, *in Ev. Matt.* xv, 33, goes off into some of his wilder allegorizings, but sees that the five callings are five world-ages. It is curious that Augustine does not use the parable to support his five world-ages, *De Civ. Dei*, XXII, 30, 5, but the interpretation suggested appears in St Ambrose (*in Ev. Luc.* VII, 223; cf. VIII, 95) and St Gregory the Great, *Hom.* 19 (Migne, *P.L.* LXXVI, col. 1155).

No doubt the original parable was intended to teach that reward is a free gift of God, not a reward of merit, and that therefore He has a right to admit the publican no less than the Pharisee to the kingdom of God (cf. Smith, *Parables*, p. 184). But it was probably in a simpler form with two, or at most three, callings to work in the vineyard. As it stands there is a certain inconsequence in the fact that it is only those who were employed first who complain of not receiving more than those called at the eleventh hour; at least those called at the third hour should have started to complain. This is the result of the complication introduced by harmonizing the parable to a conventional scheme of world-ages. If, as is probable, the original parable had three classes of labourers, Matthew, or a predecessor, only needed to insert the very colourless verse 5.

cluding aphorism which drives it home, in Luke's source for the parables of the unjust judge, the Pharisee and the publican, and the pounds (cf. above, p. 110). Nor do we find such concluding aphorisms in the collection of parables in Matt. xiii. It would seem that it was the introductory and concluding aphorisms of his collection of three parables which suggested to Matthew the idea of finding one for the parable of the wedding guests, although it was not really appropriate. Thus it seems probable that we have in these three parables an original unit, which Matthew has broken up. The parable of the unmerciful servant was obviously a suitable pendant to the saying on forgiveness; the parable of the labourers in the vineyard dealt with the theme that the last shall be first and the first last, which was suitable in the Marcan context which Matthew has been reproducing up to xix. 30 (= Mark x. 31), while the parable of the ten virgins, when translated into futurist eschatology, came in well after the Marcan apocalypse.

The remaining two parables peculiar to Matthew (the parables of the two sons, xxi. 28 ff., and of the sheep and the goats, xxv. 30 ff., which is scarcely to be classed with the others in any event) show no sign of coming from any common source. Neither has any formal introduction; and this is a peculiarity which they share with the parable of the talents in xxv. 14 ff. This absence of introductions in the three parables is remarkable in view of the elaborate openings provided by Matthew even to the quite brief parables of Matthew xiii. But this is the extent of the kinship between them. Otherwise the parables are very different in length, and have no common subject-matter or verbal association to bring them together, so that it is extremely improbable that they reached Matthew as a single tract.

In sum, Matthew's method of treating his sources makes it difficult to analyse out any further tracts of the type postulated in this study. It might be argued that in the Petrine stories of Matthew we have a collection which was originally united. There is no *a priori* reason why stories about the leader of the Twelve should not have been gathered together, and that a tract containing tales of his supernatural doings lies behind Acts ix. 31 ff. is likely enough.[1] Such a tract telling of the πράξεις Πέτρου, leading up to the climax

---

[1] Cf. my *Acts of the Apostles*, pp. 32 ff.

of the narrative of Cornelius' conversion, is exactly the sort of document that might well have circulated in circles especially interested in the thorny question of the attitude of Peter towards the Gentile mission. But it is difficult to discern any evidence that the stories about Peter in the First Gospel were ever united in any comparable way.

But it may not be merely a matter of the submergence of the sources in the general structure of Matthew's work. If the results of the present investigation are on the whole meagre so far as Matthew is concerned, that may indeed be because through historical circumstances the author of the First Gospel did not dispose of so much of the primitive tract-material as was accessible to both Mark and Luke at first hand.

THE PROBLEM OF AUTHENTICITY

Form-criticism has been in the main concerned on the one hand with the classification of the various units of the Gospel narratives and on the other hand with the valuable insight that it was not the evangelists' primary intention to give historical biographies of Jesus. Nothing in the present study necessarily tells against this latter point, which is beyond doubt justified. Nevertheless, the recognition of the 'theological' as opposed to the 'historical' purposes of the evangelists may lead to a treatment of the synoptists as ingenious artists in religious symbolism, founded upon an uncriticized presupposition that their theological purpose is of far greater significance than the historical information about events in the life of Jesus which they also give. If the present study has often had occasion to be critical of the methods and arguments employed in some form-critical work, that is partly because it seeks in some degree to represent an approach which goes beyond rather than behind form-criticism. The older liberal criticism normally assumed that the evangelists primarily intended to convey historical information about Jesus, *or at any rate that they ought to have done so* (an assumption with consequences for the liberal valuation of the Fourth Gospel). Form-criticism has undermined that assumption. Yet logically at least there is no reason why the admission of the theological interests and designs of the evangelists should lead to historical scepticism. There is much that the evangelists can tell us of the life and ministry of Jesus without its being their intention to do so. We have frequently noted instances where the synoptists seem to preserve historical information as it were by accident rather than by design. It is a curious *non sequitur* to argue, as is sometimes done, that, because the evangelists were not first and foremost interested in writing 'straight history', the Gospels contain no history, or that we cannot hope to find criteria for discerning the history in them.

Among the avowed interests of the present study, as of almost all studies of the history of the synoptic tradition in modern times, has been 'the quest of the historical Jesus'. Yet the questions of historicity and authenticity cannot be usefully discussed before the closest detective work has been done on the synoptic sources. In this book it is claimed that with admittedly varying degrees of probability, yet without relapse into airy speculation, it is still possible to trace the use by the evangelists, notably Mark and Luke, of short tracts telling of the ministry of Jesus, such as would be required by individual missionaries sent out by the primitive Christian centres, Jerusalem and Antioch. For their work the single pericope with its isolated and often anecdotal character would scarcely be adequate. On the other hand we are not postulating circumstances where the full Gospel story is needed for sustained reading or for liturgical usage. The stage here envisaged was no doubt early. Probably even in the late thirties, and certainly by the early fifties of the first century, shorter tracts of the type postulated would have become the normal type of Christian propagandist literature. Although several of these tracts were put together by Mark, there were several others which were not available to him and were used in different ways by Matthew and Luke; to these applies the symbol 'Q'.

But if the first appearance of the narratives in written form is thus likely to be at a far earlier date than it seems conventional to suppose, this does not of course settle the problems of authenticity, even if it may vastly diminish the probability of Hellenistic Christian communities or church leaders having invented much of the Gospel narratives out of their own head. From time to time it has been found possible to discern extremely primitive historical material embedded in the tradition, either because of inconsistency with any ideas which the Church of the next generation held or because of angularity and slovenliness in the workmanship of the compilers.

Nevertheless, when all the possible detective work has been done, our judgement of the value of the sources of the synoptic tradition must depend largely on the inherent content of the material and above all on the extent to which we ascribe to Jesus a 'Messianic self-consciousness'.[1] It is of course open to us to deny this entirely,

[1] Pertinent comments are made by F. C. Grant, 'The Authenticity of Jesus' Sayings', in *Neutestamentliche Studien f. Bultmann* (1954), pp. 137–43.

though this can only be done at the cost of assuming not only the almost total unreliability of the synoptic tradition, but also that in speaking of a Messianic self-consciousness we are dealing with a conception capable of precise logical definition. Thus Bultmann (p. 145) considers that 'if Jesus really knew himself to be the Messiah ... there are only two possibilities: (1) He knew himself as "the son of David" (in which case one would assume that his assertion would be met by a criticism of his ancestry, of which there is no trace), or (2) he knew himself to be the "Son of Man". . . . But this could only be understood in the sense in which Reitzenstein conceives it: Jesus knew himself as the emissary of God, who goes in humility about the earth, brings back to God by his life and teaching those who have gone astray, and waits for his exaltation. . . . But this conception of Reitzenstein seems to me to break down on account of the fact that one would then have to ascribe to Jesus a consciousness of pre-existence, of which the synoptic tradition knows nothing, and of the fact that the expectation of his exaltation is not ascribed to the historical Jesus.'

With regard to the first objection it must be pointed out that belief in the Davidic descent of Jesus is as old as Rom. i. 3 and it is at least possible that the reason why there was no criticism of his birth was that in fact he was descended from David, or at least that his family was supposed to be of Davidic origin.[1] The second involves the rejection of the passage Matt. xi. 25–7 (=Luke x. 21–2) on the ground that while the first two verses are Aramaic in origin and come from a lost Jewish original (so that possibly they are genuine), the first has the ring of Hellenistic 'revelation-literature' (Bultmann, pp. 171 f.). This ignores the fact that the specific conception of revelation and knowledge of God in this literature is admittedly drawn not from the Greek side of the Hellenistic view of religion but from the Oriental, and that Judaism was, to say the least of it, prominent among the Oriental religions which emphasized the 'knowledge of God' drawn from 'revelation' as superseding the search for God by methods of reason characteristic of

---

[1] Cf. Hegesippus, quoted by Eusebius, *H.E.* III, 20, where it is implied that the family was held to be of Davidic origin and claimed to be so. The story may not be above suspicion, but there is no necessary reason for rejecting it in view of its entirely sober and pedestrian character.

Greek thought (cf. my *Hellenistic Elements*, p. 6). Further it involves the rejection of the sayings which begin with 'I came' or 'I am sent' on the ground that while some of them may be compatible with a natural expression of Jesus' sense of his calling, yet on the whole they can be interpreted as looking back to his mission from the point of view of the later community. This is of course a purely *a priori* objection; the sayings as a whole are not seriously open to objection.[1]

It further implies that Reitzenstein's concept is the only possible alternative to the belief in Davidic sonship. Unfortunately it is by no means certain that the Mandean beliefs on which Reitzenstein bases his view are not drawn from the Christian conception of Jesus, and it is almost certain that they are post-Christian.[2] That this was roughly the conception of the primitive Church concerning the person of Jesus needs no argument. On the other hand the primitive Church, while it may well have rationalized Jesus' own conception of his mission, may quite well have done so on the whole correctly. To distinguish as Bultmann does between a 'Messianic consciousness' and a 'prophetic consciousness' as if the two were clearly distinct and mutually exclusive forms of thought assumes that there was in Judaism a consistent view of what the Messiah ought to be and that Jesus must either have held that view and identified himself with it, or alternatively have been conscious of himself only as a prophet. The first assumption is certainly incorrect; it is impossible from Jewish apocalyptic to gain any fixed and definite Messianic doctrine (cf. Moore, *Judaism*, II, pp. 323 ff.). The second assumption is certainly alien to the whole synoptic tradition, which in this respect is entirely in keeping with Jewish methods of thought in general. Jesus appears in the synoptic Gospels not as proclaiming himself as the Messiah in some specifiable sense, but as coming with absolute authority to set up the kingdom of God on earth, and, at any rate in the later stages of his ministry, as finding that his purpose can only be fulfilled by his death.

This concept is in at least one passage (Mark x. 45) based on the

---

[1] Naturally it is possible with reasonable ingenuity to find objections to all of them, e.g. that Mark ii. 17 b is a secondary expansion of the metaphor of the physician (p. 96). But that this is one of the hard sayings which have a primary claim to authenticity we have seen in Vol. I, p. 14, n. 1.

[2] Cf. note 3 in my *Gentiles*, pp. 212 ff.

prophecy of the suffering servant; it is embodied in his description of himself as 'the Son of Man'. Here we are faced with the difficulty of deciding whether Jesus used the term, and further, if he used it, whether he used it of himself only, or whether he distinguished between himself and the apocalyptic Son of Man who was to come in glory at the end of all things. With regard to the latter question it must be noticed that Bultmann accepts the view that Jesus distinguishes himself from the eschatological Son of Man (p. 117 on Matt. x. 32 f. as against Luke xii. 8 and Mark viii. 38, and p. 128 on Luke xvii. 22 f.). The identification is due to the evangelists. Here it must be noted that the distinction between Jesus and the Son of Man can only be held to be original if it be assumed that in these two passages we have a version so close to the original words of Jesus that we can rely on them for evidence that there was a tradition older than the evangelists which preserved an original distinction, which they have forgotten or ignored. The case for such a view is distinctly weakened by the fact that the distinction can equally well be drawn in such a verse as Mark xiv. 62, which Bultmann holds to be 'a secondary expansion of the short account of xv. 1'. (It has been seen in Vol. 1, pp. 131 ff. that the account is drawn by Mark from a source which is different from and inferior to his source for xv. 1.) We may compare Matt. xix. 28 where the same distinction can be made; but since the saying is treated as a saying of the risen Christ, emanating from the early Jewish Church (Bultmann, p. 171), Matthew clearly here means 'Jesus as the Son of Man' and has not in mind the original distinction between the two. This necessity of explaining away passages where the Son of Man can be distinguished from Jesus just as well as in Matt. x. 32 f. and Luke xvii. 23 f. throws a considerable doubt on the attempt to show that in those two passages we have an original distinction preserved, the more so as the Lucan apocalypse is open to the suspicion of being an adaptation of Jewish matter (see above, p. 109); in any event the verse, coming as it does immediately after the certainly authentic refusal to give a date for the Second Coming in xvii. 20 ff., is open to suspicion (Creed *ad loc.*; the verse is peculiar to Luke and perhaps originates with him). Similarly while it is possible that the change of 'the Son of Man' in Mark viii. 38 and Luke x. 8 to 'I' in Matt. xii. 8 is due to mere carelessness on the part of Matthew, it is also possible that he has preserved the original text. Creed on the Lucan passage points out that 'the Son of Man' here is not judge but advocate.

The difficulties surrounding the term would appear to be due for the most part to the assumption that the phrase must from the first have been used by Jesus in a definite sense, which was clear alike to himself and to his hearers from the beginning. The assumption is certainly not necessary; it is doubtful whether it is even probable.[1] The phrase falls into line with the language of the Messianic pretenders who are a feature of the history of Judaea at this time. Thus Theudas 'proclaimed himself to be somebody'.[2] Both he and 'the Egyptian' (Jos. *Antt.* xx, 97 ff. and 167 ff.) seem to have implied that they were Joshua (or Jesus?) returning to set up a Messianic kingdom, since Theudas proposed to lead his followers dryshod across the Jordan and the Egyptian to cause the walls of Jerusalem to fall down flat.[3] Simon of Samaria called himself (or allowed himself to be called) 'the Great Power of God', while Bar Cochba's name means 'the son of a star'. In spite of the complete difference between Jesus and men of this class the problem that confronted them was the same, in so far as they had to collect followers without immediately attracting the hostile attention of the Romans and the rulers of the Jews. In the case of Jesus we have further to recognize that for his purpose it was essential to draw men to hear the proclamation of the kingdom of God and to see in it the fulfilment of the hope of Israel while at the same time renouncing the whole conception of a worldly kingdom to be set up by force. For this purpose an enigmatic title which suggested that he was the fulfilment of the hope of Israel was almost essential if he was to gain a hearing, while among those who heard him it would invest him with an authority which might reconcile them to the abandonment of all their ambitions.[4] The fact that similarly ambiguous phrases

[1] Cf. W. Manson, *Jesus the Messiah*, p. 16, for the suggestion that 'what we call the Messianic consciousness of Jesus registers not the starting-point but rather the climax of his self-expression, the moment of highest tension in the unfolding of his sense of destiny'.

[2] Acts v. 36. The difficulties of the passage do not concern us; the point is that the story goes back to a source which found the description natural.

[3] Cf. my *Hellenistic Elements*, p. 26.

[4] The ambiguity of the title and its effect on the hearers seem to be correctly estimated in such passages as John x. 24 and xii. 34. It is not to be supposed that

were used by 'false Christs' does not rule out the possibility that Jesus used a similar phrase, since the need for such a phrase was partly conditioned by the circumstances of the time in which he lived and partly by the conditions of his mission.

This explanation avoids the difficulty which arises when the term is confined to any particular sense, while it further explains the fact that in some cases it appears to have been extended beyond the sense in which it was originally used by Jesus. Thus it might be used of the purely eschatological figure of the Son of Man coming on the clouds of heaven. Exactly how far Jesus' eschatology was purely concerned with the irruption of the kingdom of God into this world in a manner which implied a future vindication of himself and his disciples, and how far on the other hand his mind was coloured by the current eschatology of his time, is a matter which can hardly be determined; but it must be remembered that the circumstances of that time were such as to lead almost inevitably to the expansion and misinterpretation of his words in an eschatological sense.[1] The misinterpretation would be easier if 'the Son of Man' was a concept which was deliberately left to the interpretation of the hearers. On the other hand it might be substituted for the phrase 'son of man' in the sense of 'man as such'; it is at least probable that this has happened.[2]

the scenes are historical, but they would appear to reflect accurately the effect which the phrase would have on a Jewish audience. From this point of view it becomes otiose to inquire whether we are to interpret the phrase on the lines of Ezekiel (i.e. = 'man') but as applied to a particular prophet, or of Daniel (= a personification of Israel which is also their angelic ruler), or as a Messianic figure, as in I Enoch xlvi. 2, assuming this part of Enoch to be pre-Christian. For the possibility that the reinterpretation of Daniel by Jesus is independent of Enoch cf. Dodd, *Parables*, p. 83.

[1] Cf. Dodd, *Parables*, pp. 88 ff. In general I am in entire agreement with his conception of the eschatology of Jesus, though I am inclined to suspect that there was a rather larger element of futurist eschatology, in the sense of a looking forward to a future vindication of his mission by a final act of God in bringing the process of history to an end, than he seems to allow.

[2] Cf. Str.-B. *ad loc.* Bultmann (*Gesch.*, p. 109) objects to the argument that this and similar sayings of Jesus may be genuine on the ground that 'one must recognise that many words owe their acceptance into the tradition only to their suitability for a particular connection'. But the question can only be decided on the grounds of a general view of the reliability or unreliability of the tradition as a whole. If we start with the assumption of its unreliability we can explain almost any saying away by finding a situation in the life of the Church which might have led to the inclusion, modification or invention of a proverbial saying of this type. On the other hand the

Naturally it is impossible to say precisely what may have been consciously present to the mind of Jesus on any particular occasion. But the attempt to confine his mind within the limits of a 'prophetic' as opposed to a 'Messianic' self-consciousness, in so far as it means anything, leaves no real explanation of the opposition he aroused, as compared with the Baptist.[1] Further, we have to assume that the appearance of Jesus in the non-Marcan tradition involves a modification of Q (for which Jesus was not the Messiah) by a Jewish wing of the Hellenistic community which was interested in Messianic ideals while the Greeks were not (Bultmann, p. 330). For such modification by a Jewish wing of the Hellenistic community there is of course no evidence; and our knowledge of Hellenistic Judaism seems to show that it was little interested in Messianic speculation (cf. my *Hellenistic Elements*, p. 40). Moreover, such passages as Matt. xi. 2–19 (= Luke vii. 18–35) show Jesus quite clearly as the inaugurator of the Messianic age; it is possible to ascribe them to early controversies between the Church and the followers of the Baptist (Bultmann, p. 22), but it must be remembered that our only knowledge of such controversies, and of the Baptist's disciples after their master's death, rests on the problematic Acts xix. 1 ff., and a quite dubious inference from John i. 19 ff. and iii. 22 ff.[2]

Gospels present the use of popular proverbial sayings, with or without a modification to the particular conditions, as a regular part of the method of teaching employed by Jesus. In this case we have, if we reject the saying, to suppose that it was first introduced into the tradition in the rabbinical sense and then misunderstood as referring not to man as such but to Jesus as the Son of Man.

[1] Cf. Josephus, *Antt.* XVIII, 117, where the statement that the pious Jews approved of the Baptist is the only probable statement in the whole story.

[2] Bultmann (p. 23, note) is rightly sceptical of Reitzenstein's view that the Q passage referred to above has any connexion with the Mandean accounts of the Baptist. The Johannine passages might be due to controversies between the Church and the followers of the Baptist, if they ever formed anything in the nature of a coherent community, for which we have too little evidence. It is at least curious that the controversy should play so large a part in the Fourth Gospel unless we allow it a much earlier date than seems at all probable. The Johannine passages may equally well be intended to show that John was the prophesied forerunner of the Messiah (cf. Justin Martyr, *Dial.* 49: John was not indeed Elijah, but he was the counterpart of Elijah sent to prepare for the first coming of Jesus). We can of course suppose that the story of Acts xix. 1 is Luke's way of glossing over a serious and lasting controversy between the Church and a Johannine community at Ephesus which has left its mark on the Fourth Gospel; but it is a somewhat temerarious inference from a very small body of evidence. Cf. also p. 41, above.

The view that the term 'Son of Man' was deliberately chosen by
Jesus to force his hearers to ask themselves exactly what his message
meant and what the kingdom of God which he established was
intended to be is consistent with the much discussed 'Messianic
secret' in Mark. As the injunctions to secrecy stand in the Gospel
they make no sense at all; Jesus in Mark i. 43 ff. forbids a leper
to say anything of his cure, while in Mark i. 34 and iii. 12 he
refuses to allow the devils to recognize him. In Mark vii. 36 'they'
(apparently several people whose cures had been related in the same
source; cf. Vol. I, p. 60) are told to say nothing to anyone, while
in viii. 35 the blind man is told not even to enter the village. As
against this the miracles of feeding are performed in circumstances
which would make any kind of secrecy impossible; in Mark v. 43
the parents are told to say nothing, although it is perfectly clear
from verse 38 that the death of the daughter of Jairus was known to a
large number of people and that her raising from the dead could not
be concealed. There is a continual clash between the *motif* of con-
cealment and the acclamations common to miracle-stories. But if we
grant that Jesus did not want to be recognized specifically as the
Messiah on the strength of his healings of particular cases of possession, or on other occasions when an outburst of popular enthusiasm
would have produced inconveniences of one kind or another
(including possibly the hostile attention of the Roman government),
while on other occasions his healings of disease were performed in
circumstances in which publicity was unavoidable (as in the case of
Bartimaeus), we have a reasonable explanation of the data. Mark
has no doubt exaggerated the injunctions to secrecy, as in v. 43 (the
prohibition in viii. 26 comes in a story of a primitive type, and may
perfectly well preserve a historical fact, namely, that Jesus told the
man just healed to go straight home, since he did not wish at the
moment to attract attention; by the next day or so Jesus would
presumably have gone elsewhere). On the other hand the miracle-
stories included an acclamation as a regular feature and we have a
very unsuccessful attempt to combine them in Mark vii. 36.[1]

[1] I cannot agree with the generally received view (cf. Dibelius, *Formgesch. d.
Evang.*[2], p. 225) that the passages in question reveal the 'pragmatism' of Mark's
Gospel as showing 'that Jesus did not wish himself to be honoured as a miracle-
worker and to make it plain how, in spite of so many proofs of his supernatural
power, he was not recognized as the Messiah'. I cannot believe that he was capable

Similar considerations explain the incident of the triumphal entry into Jerusalem (Mark xi. 1 ff.). Bultmann (p. 281) may well be right in regarding the apparently miraculous knowledge of Jesus as to the whereabouts of the ass as a legendary feature; his dismissal of the presuppositions of the story, namely 'that Jesus wished to enact the fulfilment of Zech. ix. 9 and that the crowd immediately recognized the ass as a Messianic mount', as 'absurd' comes dangerously near to using a bludgeon in the place of an argument. That Jesus should enter in circumstances which deliberately challenged the bystanders to face the question whether he was the Messiah or not, by doing it in a way which could call to mind the prophecy of Zechariah, seems perfectly possible when it is remembered how vague the Messianic idea was and the extent to which the period was excited by various Messianic hopes.[1] The fact that legendary features may have been intruded into the story need not mean that the story as a whole (which is admitted to rest on the historical fact of the entry of Jesus escorted by a crowd looking forward to the imminent coming of the kingdom of God) has been transformed into a Messianic legend. It is possible that the legendary features are due to a misunderstanding of the last clause of Mark xi. 3. The words may equally well be translated: 'say "The master needs him and will send him back at once"', or 'say "The master needs him" and he (the owner) will send him back at once'.[2] It is quite possible that in the original version the words bore the first meaning, but that the ambiguity led to the enlargement of the story by the legendary feature of the foreknowledge of Jesus and the statement that no one as yet had ever sat on the colt.

of this extremely subtle technique, especially in view of the fact that he himself is completely puzzled by the stupidity of the disciples at viii. 14 ff. It seems far more likely that the tradition rightly recorded such prohibitions of the publication of cures, which may have become in some cases conventional features. On the other hand other stories ended with a conventional acclamation and the two had somehow to be reconciled as in vii. 36 f. Dibelius' second point may apply, however, to ix. 9 and possibly, though not necessarily, to viii. 30 which may well be historical.

[1] From the point of view of nineteenth-century Liberalism such a challenge might seem 'absurd'; but from the same point of view it would seem no less absurd for Jeremiah to buy a potter's earthen vessel and take the elders of the people and of the priests to 'the valley of the son of Hinnon' and break the vessel there in their presence as a sign of the destruction of Jerusalem.

[2] I owe the suggestion to Professor C. H. Dodd.

It will be observed that the views put forward above imply that the predictions of the Passion in Mark viii. 31, ix. 30 ff. and x. 32 ff., though apparently drawn from good sources, are not historical in so far as they record an explicit forecast of a resurrection on the third day; it is not likely that the detailed predictions of the Passion were delivered in their present form. On the other hand there is no reason to doubt that Jesus foresaw his death as, humanly speaking, the certain result of his journey to Jerusalem and coupled it with an expression of his certain confidence that God would vindicate him. This has been rewritten in the light of the events, whatever they may have been, which led the disciples to believe that the Lord had risen. The extent to which that rewriting was legitimate depends on the extent to which their belief was justified.

APPENDIX

THE OXYRHYNCHUS SAYINGS

This appendix was written before the announcement of the discovery by Professor H. C. Puech that the *Gospel of Thomas* found in the 'gnostic' library of Nag-Hammadi consists of a complete collection of the Sayings of Jesus, and that its beginning corresponds with P. Oxy. 654. I have thought it best to leave the text as it stands on the ground that even if the conclusions may now be questioned, much of the detailed argument may retain its validity; and in any event there seems little hope of early publication of the Nag-Hammadi text.

The collections of sayings ascribed to Jesus in P. Oxy. 1 and P. Oxy. 654[1] have no serious claim to be regarded as authentic except in so far as they contain sayings drawn from the synoptic tradition, or possibly from some variant form of it now lost. That the sayings have an impressive and edifying ring about them may be granted; but the decisive point is the Hellenistic character of the material for which the synoptic Gospels provide no parallel.

The Hellenistic stamp of the non-synoptic matter is beyond doubt in the third 'logion' of P. Oxy. 1 (in Evelyn White's edition, Saying VIII, p. 31):

Λέγει 'Ι(ησοῦ)ς· ἔ[σ]την
ἐν μέσῳ τοῦ κόσμου
καὶ ἐν σαρκεὶ ὤφθην
αὐτοῖς καὶ εὖρον πάν-
τας μεθύοντας καὶ
οὐδένα εὖρον δειψῶ(ν)-
τα ἐν αὐτοῖς· καὶ πο-
νεῖ ἡ ψυχή μου ἐπὶ
τοῖς υἱοῖς τῶν ἀν(θρώπ)ων,
ὅτι τυφλοί εἰσιν τῇ καρ-
δίᾳ αὐτῶ[ν] καὶ οὐ βλέπ-
[ουσιν . . .

[1] The most convenient edition remains that of H. G. Evelyn White, *The Sayings of Jesus from Oxyrhynchus* (Cambridge, 1920).

149

Jeremias has recently argued, not unreasonably, that the saying has some Semitic marks, the parataxis in the first half being marked, and the last half being reminiscent not only of synoptic language such as the lament over Jerusalem (Matt. xxiii. 37–9; Luke xii. 34–5) or Mark ix. 19 but also of Isa. liii. 10 (the travail of his soul). He thinks the saying is 'mixed', being 'gnostic' in its opening phrases (though it is in these that the parataxis is apparent), and 'synoptic' in tone in the more important latter half.[1]

But the parataxis seems quite self-conscious; it is being used as a means of creating a solemn and hieratic effect.[2] That the first part of the saying may not come from the same background as the second part may be allowed; the change of tense may be added to Jeremias' arguments. And that the 'gnostic' milieu of the first part is heretical seems improbable in view of the undocetic ἐν σαρκὶ ὤφθην which points to Johannine influence. Be that as it may, the language of καὶ εὖρον πάντας μεθύοντας κτλ. is drawn from the type of Hellenistic preaching summoning men from the drunkenness of ignorance to the sobriety of truth, which may go back to 'Orphic' missionaries of the classical period but which was in any event common among Greeks and Jews at the beginning of the Christian era.[3] Moreover, it is the risen Christ who here speaks in the past tense of his incarnation as a sad and disappointing episode. This is far from the synoptic picture.

In the fifth 'logion' of P. Oxy. 1 (Saying x in Evelyn White: 'lift the stone and thou shalt find me, cleave the wood and there I am') Jesus is made to represent himself as the divine element permeating the cosmos in all its parts—in other words, the Wisdom-Logos of Pauline and Johannine theology is equated absolutely with the Stoic element of divinity which penetrates all things and gives them their nature and place in the harmony of things.[4] C. Taylor objects that if this is the sense there is no point in lifting the stone

---

[1] Joachim Jeremias, *Unbekannte Jesusworte* (Gütersloh, 1951), pp. 67–70.

[2] Cf. *The Gospel of Eve* ap. Epiph. *Panarion*, XXVI, 3, 1: ἔστην ἐπὶ ὄρους ὑψηλοῦ καὶ εἶδον ἄνθρωπον μακρὸν καὶ ἄλλον κολοβόν, καὶ ἤκουσα ὡσεὶ φωνὴν βροντῆς καὶ ἤγγισα τοῦ ἀκοῦσαι καὶ ἐλάλησε πρός με καὶ εἶπεν· ἐγὼ σὺ καὶ σὺ ἐγώ, καὶ ὅπου ἐὰν ᾖς ἐγὼ ἐκεῖ εἰμι, καὶ ἐν ἅπασίν εἰμι ἐσπαρμένος.

[3] Cf. Knox, *Gentiles*, p. 38, n. 4.

[4] Diog. Laert. VII, 138; cf. Origen, *in Ev. Joann.* I, 30, 154, and Bevan, *Stoics and Sceptics*, pp. 42 f.

or cutting the wood.[1] This seems hypercritical, the point being that we find the divine element of mind in everyday things as treated in the actions of daily life. More ingenious perhaps is the argument of Jeremias[2] that the saying is a counterblast to the cynicism of Eccles. x. 9, and means that in all their toil Jesus' presence with his disciples saves them from frustration. The first part of the saying ('where one is alone I say that I am with him') might be a logical completion of Matt. xviii. 20, a Christian version of *Pirke Aboth*, III, 2. It might equally well be the Hellenistic commonplace that no man is deserted since God cares for all.[3] The affinities of the saying as a whole appear to be with the pantheistic mysticism of such passages as the fragment from the *Gospel of Eve* (quoted above, p. 150, n. 2) or *Corp. Herm.* V, 11:[4] σὺ γὰρ εἶ ὃ ἂν ὦ, σὺ εἶ ὃ ἂν ποιῶ, σὺ εἶ ὃ ἂν λέγω. σὺ γὰρ πάντα εἶ καὶ ἄλλο οὐδὲν ἔστιν· ὃ μὴ ἔστι, σὺ εἶ.

The second collection of P. Oxy. 654 has similar affinities. In the first 'logion' ('Let him who seeks cease not until he finds, and when he finds he shall be astonished; astonished he shall reign and having reigned he shall rest'), which is quoted by Clement of Alexandria once as from the Gospel according to the Hebrews (*Strom.* II, 45, 5) and a second time without the source being named (*Strom.* V, 96, 3), if 'rest' and 'reign' come from the Christian tradition, the idea of 'wonder' is Hellenistic. That wonder is the beginning of philosophy goes back to Plato, *Theaet.* 155 f. (cf. Stallbaum's note *ad loc.*), and appears in Philo, *de Praem. et Poen.* 34 (τὴν τῶν ὅλων φύσιν ἀεὶ θαυμαστέον), *Corp. Herm.* IV, 5, where it leads to the apprehension of God, and especially in the remarkably close parallel of *Corp. Herm.* XIV, 4, where wonder is the second of successive stages by which we advance to recognize our true father; here the parallel is one of form as well as of content: οὕτως ἐστὶν ἄξιον νοῆσαι καὶ νοήσαντα θαυμάσαι καὶ θαυμάσαντα ἑαυτὸν μακαρίσαι, τὸν πατέρα γνωρίσαντα. In *Corp. Herm.* XIII, 20 the hymn of wondering admiration ends in 'rest'.

A similarly Hellenistic colouring appears in the second 'logion'

---

[1] *The Oxyrhynchus Logia*, p. 40.   [2] *Op. cit.* pp. 88 ff.
[3] Philo, *de Spec. Legg.* I, 308 ff.; cf. *Hellenistic Elements*, p. 79.
[4] Parallel material from the Hellenistic underworld is collected in Festugière's note on this passage in his edition.

(Saying II in Evelyn White), the restoration of which is problematic. For convenience Schubart's reconstruction is reproduced here.[1]

λέγει Ἰ[ησοῦς· λέγουσιν
οἱ ἕλκοντες ἡμᾶς [εἰς τὸν κόσμον ὅτι
ἡ βασιλεία ἐν οὐρα[νῷ ἐστιν. ἐλέγχει δὲ
τὰ πετεινὰ τοῦ οὐρ[ανοῦ καὶ πᾶν ζῷον ὅ-
τι ὑπὸ τὴν γῆν ἐστ[ιν ἢ ἐπὶ τῆς γῆς καὶ
οἱ ἰχθύες τῆς θαλά[σσης πάντες ὁδηγοῦν-
τες ὑμᾶς. καὶ ἡ βασ[ιλεία τῶν οὐρανῶν
ἐντὸς ὑμῶν [ἐ]στι, [καὶ ὅστις ἂν ἑαυτὸν
γνῷ, ταύτην εὑρή[σει. μέλλοντες δὲ
ἑαυτοὺς γνώσεσθαι [εἰδήσετε ὅτι υἱοί
ἐστε ὑμεῖς τοῦ πατρὸς τοῦ τ[ελείου. ὅλως δὲ
γνώ⟨σε⟩σθε ἑαυτοὺς ἐν [τῇ πτώσει τοῦ κόσμου
καὶ ὑμεῖς ἐστε ἡ πτῶ[σις.

Schubart (following C. Taylor) is no doubt right in finding the key to the reconstruction in Job xii. 7 LXX, whatever doubts may be aroused by his suggestions for lines 2–3 and for the ending. The main point is thoroughly Hellenistic. The saying 'The kingdom of God is within you' has become a mystery of *gnosis*, and the initiate's ascent is achieved by introspective self-knowledge. This is all closely reminiscent of the Valentinian exposition of the content of *gnosis* in *Excerpta ex Theodoto*, 78, or the fragmentary note in Clement, *Ecl. Proph.* 17.

Accordingly the content of the Oxyrhynchus sayings shows that they come from a Hellenistic milieu; the question of their form and origin must now be discussed. The papyri present us with a form similar to that which we have traced in many of the collections behind the synoptic Gospels: a narrative introduction of a formal kind (it is preserved in P. Oxy. 654, but the opening of P. Oxy. 1 has been lost), followed by a string of sayings. In P. Oxy. 654 we have the further similarity of a stupid question being put by the disciples in order to elicit a further saying. The formula which introduces the sayings, λέγει Ἰησοῦς, is admittedly more reminiscent of Johannine than of synoptic usage; the historical present is pre-

---

[1] W. Schubart, 'Das zweite Logion Oxyrhynchus Pap. IV 654', in *Zeits. f. d. neutest. Wiss.* XX (1921), pp. 215–23.

sumably used because this has become the recognized hieratic language of the Church.

Much of the discussion concerning the source of the fragments has proceeded on the assumption that they must either be drawn from an apocryphal gospel now lost or else have a high claim to be regarded as authentic sayings. The latter view cannot be maintained in view of their Hellenistic character; on the other hand it is by no means certain that they ever formed part of a gospel. Q has even been suggested! The question of their origin is to some extent bound up with that of their date; Grenfell and Hunt held that, being a fragment of a book and having abbreviations of the *nomina sacra*, P. Oxy. 1 could not be dated earlier than the third century, P. Oxy. 654 being a few decades later. But it now appears that these features are compatible with an earlier date (cf. Bell and Skeat, *Fragments of an Unknown Gospel*, pp. 2 ff.). The Codex containing the 'Unknown Gospel' is given a date of about A.D. 150 on what the editors regard as a very cautious estimate; if so, it seems that non-canonical centos, drawn largely from the canonical Gospels, were current during the middle of the second century.[1] Thus it is perfectly possible that we have in these two Oxyrhynchus fragments an early compilation of sayings (which may or may not have been a gospel), made about the middle of the second century, which was not identical with any of the known apocryphal gospels. The purpose of the compilation appears to be that of the Fourth Gospel, in so far as the latter is an attempt to state the authentic Palestinian tradition in terms of Hellenistic thought, though we have no reason to suppose that the compiler possessed either the spiritual insight or the literary genius of the fourth evangelist. As regards the date of the original composition

[1] In the 'Unknown Gospel' the verbal resemblance (almost amounting to identity) between lines 7–14 and John v. 39 and 45, and the close similarity between the story of the leper and that in Mark i. 40 ff. with parallels (the insertion being simply intended to explain why this one leper was cleansed), seem conclusive evidence that we are dealing with a cento. Note that the rare Marcan ἐμβριμησάμενος has been transferred to the story of the tribute-money. The synoptic parallels might of course be due to the fact that the writer of the 'Unknown Gospel' was drawing on the same material as the Synoptic writers; but the Johannine extracts are taken from a typically Johannine argument with the Jews: I cannot agree with the editors' first opinion (admittedly much modified in the popular pamphlet subsequently issued by the British Museum Trustees, *The New Gospel Fragments*, 1935) that there is any serious reason to hold that the compiler is drawing on independent tradition.

of these collections of sayings, it is fairly clear that the writer of P. Oxy. 1 knew Luke. He has preserved the Lucan form of the saying about the mote and the beam (Luke vi. 42 c) except that he puts ἐκβαλεῖν immediately after διαβλέψεις as in Matthew instead of at the end, but there is fairly strong manuscript support for reading the sentence in Luke as in P. Oxy. 1. Similarly he preserves the Lucan form of the saying at Nazareth, 'No prophet is acceptable in his own country'. It is of course possible that both Luke and the papyrus here are following an independent tradition;[1] but the double resemblance, together with the appearance in P. Oxy. 654 of the Lucan saying 'The kingdom of heaven' (Luke reads 'God', but 'heaven' is an almost certain restoration in the papyrus) 'is within you', strongly favours the view that the compiler knew Luke; since it is not likely that he knew Luke alone of the synoptists it is probable that in P. Oxy. 1 we have an amplification of Matt. xviii. 20. Further, the prologue to P. Oxy. 654 implies a knowledge of the Fourth Gospel, in view of the quotation of John viii. 52 and the appearance of Thomas (cf. Evelyn White, *op. cit.* p. 4). Thus even after the composition of the four Gospels it was possible for apparently orthodox Christians to make up such compilations of texts consisting in part of sayings from the Gospels, in part of amplifications and amendments by the compiler.[2] The circulation of the canonical Gospels in the Church would naturally tend to eliminate unofficial collections and to prevent further compilations of this kind. New and heretical gospels might appear, but the collection of sayings as a means of preserving or falsifying the teaching of the Lord would fall into disuse.

Evelyn White holds that our two papyri are drawn from different copies of the same collection, and are excerpts from the Gospel according to the Hebrews.[3] But it is equally possible that they are

[1] For the view that Luke here is dependent on a non-Marcan version cf. Vol. 1, p. 48.

[2] In all probability Papias' collection was essentially the same (Eus. *H.E.* III, 39, 11). It would seem that it contained nothing that was not in our Gospels except matter obviously not authentic.

[3] The evidence for their being drawn from the same collection is (*a*) that both use the historical present 'Jesus says'—but this may well have been a hieratic formula in use in Egypt and proves nothing; (*b*) that according to Clem. Alex. *Strom.* II, 45, 5 the first saying of P. Oxy. 654 occurs in the Gospel according to the Hebrews: for this cf. below, p. 156.

older,[1] since there is no real evidence of the early date of the Gospel according to the Hebrews. The saying ascribed to the risen Lord by Ignatius, λάβετε, ψηλαφήσατέ με καὶ ἴδετε ὅτι οὐκ εἰμὶ δαιμόνιον ἀσώματον, is said by Jerome (*De Vir. Ill.* 16) to come from the Gospel according to the Hebrews; but our trust in his statement is lessened by the fact that he misquotes the introductory words and ascribes the saying to Ignatius' letter to Polycarp, whereas it comes from his letter to the Smyrneans. Origen, on the other hand, states that the saying comes from the Preaching of Peter (*De Princ.* 1, praef. 8). The question is complicated by the fact that the Gospel according to the Hebrews is traditionally supposed to be Ebionite; according to Irenaeus the Ebionites only use Matthew (1, 26, 2), while according to Eusebius (*H.E.* III, 27, 4) they only use the Gospel according to the Hebrews. But the saying of Ignatius is not at all likely to have occurred in a Jewish-Christian gospel; the word δαιμόνιον is never used in the LXX, N.T., or in Jewish writers of the Palestinian type in its neutral sense of a disembodied spirit, but always of a 'devil'. (Cf. Förster in *T.W.ʒ.N.T.* s.v. δαίμων.) Only in Acts xvii. 22 and xxv. 19 do we get a reminiscence of the originally neutral sense of the word in the use of δεισιδαίμων. The hellenized Jews, Philo and Josephus, habitually use the word in its classical sense; but Philo at least only uses it so in passages which he is taking over from heathen writers; where he is writing as a Jew or using Jewish sources, the word is used in its regular Jewish sense of a heathen deity, who is *ex hypothesi* a 'devil'.[2]

---

[1] Grenfell and Hunt give A.D. 140 as the probable date of compilation; Evelyn White regards it as the latest possible.

[2] Thus in *De Gig.* 6 ff.=*De Somn.* 1, 141; cf. Cicero, *De Nat. Deor.* II, 15, 42, Diog. Laert. VII, 151 and Plato, *Phaedo* 114 D. In *Q.O.P.L.* 39 Philo is adapting a Stoic tract; *ibid.* 30 he is quoting a story about Theodorus 'the atheist'. In *De Aet. Mund.* 47, 64 and 76 we have the adjective used in a good sense, this tract being merely an adaptation of pagan sources. In *In Flacc.* 168 and 179 he is writing from Flaccus' point of view; in *Leg. ad G.* 65 and 112 he is incorporating a pagan Alexandrine lampoon on Caligula (cf. *Hellenistic Elements*, p. 48). On the other hand in *De Vit. Moys.* 1, 276 we read of a pillar set up to a local δαιμόνιον, and in *De Decal.* 54 we have a Jewish criticism of the attempt to justify paganism by physical allegories and here Poseidon has various δαίμονες ἐνάλιοι subject to himself. In these two passages Philo writes as a Jew or uses Jewish sources; the last need not have a bad sense in itself, but he is quoting from the current Stoic method of argument. But

There is thus a serious difficulty about supposing that this saying comes from the Gospel according to the Hebrews, if this was identical with or even akin to the Gospel of the Ebionites or that in use in Palestine as Eusebius says in his account of Hegesippus (*H.E.* IV, 22, 8). If we rule out Ignatius' evidence we have no proof that it was older than our collection, since Hegesippus, if he really used this Gospel, might have been using a compilation of about A.D. 140. Evelyn White is hardly justified in assuming that the Gospel according to the Hebrews and the Ebionite Gospel were really the same; Clement of Alexandria states that the saying 'he that wonders shall reign' comes from this Gospel, and the saying suggests Alexandria rather than Ebionite circles. In any case it is quite impossible to suppose that Ignatius' quotation was part of the Ebionite Gospel according to the Hebrews; either there were two quite distinct gospels, the Ebionite and the Alexandrine, or there was an Alexandrine recension of the Ebionite Gospel with some very Alexandrine additions. We are left with Hegesippus and Irenaeus as evidence for a Palestinian Gospel and Clement as the earliest evidence for the view that our sayings had anything in common with the Gospel according to the Hebrews whatever the document he knew may have been.

Thus it remains possible that as a literary form our collections represent a stage of tradition older than our Gospels, even if this particular collection was composed after the canonical Gospels had begun to circulate. The two, or the one if both are parts of the same document, may have been longer than the collections which, it is suggested, were used by the synoptic writers. The *verso* of P. Oxy. 1 is numbered 'eleven', but it is not certain that the ια is meant as a page number; and it is not clear that the number is that of the page of the collection rather than of the page of the book which may have contained other items. Similarly P. Oxy. 654 must have been a fairly long document if it occupied the whole back of the probably lengthy rent-roll on which it is written. But the back may have

---

he uses εὐδαίμων quite conventionally (not in LXX or N.T.). Josephus appears to be far more indiscriminate than Philo.

Christian writers normally follow New Testament usage: Tertullian maliciously interprets the δαιμόνιον of Socrates as a 'demon' in the New Testament sense (*de Anima*, 39).

contained other matter as well. Nor have we any evidence that both papyri contain parts of the same set of sayings; the only argument for this is that both stand in much the same relation to the canonical Gospels and treat them in the same way. But, apart from the gnostic collections of P. Oxy. 655 and 1224, the discovery of the 'Unknown Gospel' shows that expansions of the canonical Gospels were not unknown in orthodox circles in Egypt, and the papyri may represent two separate attempts to expand the sayings of Jesus in a rather mechanical way so as to adapt them to the popular philosophy of the Hellenistic world.

Setting aside the Hellenistic content, their form justifies the speculation that we have in them specimens of collections of the sayings of Jesus similar to the short tracts discernible behind Mark and Luke. The appearance of the canonical Gospels and the use of the gospel form by gnostic writers would naturally result in the gradual elimination of such unauthorized compilations; the two papyri discussed above would appear to be survivals of an earlier method of preaching the Gospel which was at one time accepted as the authoritative method of the Church.[1]

---

[1] It may be conjectured that the Fourth Gospel shows signs of having drawn on a similar collection at least at one point. As it stands c. x consists (*a*) of sayings reminiscent of the synoptists, dealing with the shepherd and the sheep, and (*b*) of a series of sayings on the relation of Jesus to the Father. The former (x. 1–16 with 7–9 inserted in the original tract on the principle of verbal association and 26–8) might represent an original collection of 'shepherd' sayings, with the original introduction to a new saying left in at 7 (6 being probably due to the evangelist). The latter consists of 17–18 (inserted here to carry on the thought of Jesus laying down his life for the sheep in 15), 25–6, and 29–30. (For the text and sense of 29 cf. Hoskyns and Davey *ad loc.*) The narrative and dialogue of 19–24 are inserted by the evangelist to break the monotony of the long discourse. The motive for the conflation is that the evangelist wishes to make it clear that Jesus as the good shepherd is also the divine Logos (cf. my *Hellenistic Elements*, pp. 71 ff.). Whether the shepherd collection contains original elements or is worked up from Matt. xviii. 12–14 (=Luke xv. 3–7) cannot be decided. The suggestions given above are of course only conjectural; they have the merit of explaining the peculiar structure of the passage.

INDEXES

I. GREEK AND LATIN WRITERS

II. JEWISH WRITERS

III. OLD TESTAMENT

IV. NEW TESTAMENT

V. CHRISTIAN WRITERS

VI. MODERN WRITERS